THE HILL OF DEVI

BY E. M. FORSTER

THE HILL OF DEVI

BY E. M. FORSTER

A HARVEST/HBJ BOOK

HARCOURT BRACE JOVANOVICH

NEW YORK AND LONDON

ISBN 0-15-640265-3

Library of Congress Catalog Card Number: 53-9224

PRINTED IN THE UNITED STATES OF AMERICA

TO MALCOLM

✍ PREFACE ૐ

This book has grown up round two visits which I paid
to the Indian state of Dewas Senior. The first visit
was in 1912-13, the second in 1921. The letters I wrote
home on those far-off occasions would not, by themselves, be worth publishing, but it so happens that
my knowledge of Dewas is extensive: I was more or
less in touch with its inner workings over a period of
thirty years.

The 1912-13 letters are printed without introduc-
tion in the hope that the reader may share my be-
wilderment and pleasure at plunging into an unknown
world and at meeting an unknown and possibly un-
knowable character. They are followed by an explana-
tory essay, entitled "The State and Its Ruler." Then
comes the main section, the 1921 letters, written
when I was the ruler's Private Secretary, together with
a commentary on them. Then comes the catastrophe.

Most of my letters were addressed to my mother
and to other relatives. They are, unfortunately, none
the better on that account. I was writing to people

7

of whom I was fond and whom I wanted to amuse, with the result that I became too humorous and conciliatory, and too prone to turn remote and rare matters into suburban jokes. In editing I have had to cut out a good deal of "How I wish you were all here!" or "Aren't Indians quaint!"

I did not really think the Indians quaint, and my deepest wish was to be alone with them. "Amusing letters home," from Miss Eden's onward, have their drawbacks. Aiming at freshness, they may sacrifice dignity and depth. I hope that the fineness of Dewas Senior, as well as its strangeness, may occasionally shine through. It was the great opportunity of my life.

I was introduced to the place by Malcolm Darling (now Sir M. L. Darling, K.C.I.E.). It is he who kept me in touch with it, to him I owe everything, and to him I dedicate this record of a vanished civilisation. Some will rejoice that it has vanished. Others will feel that something precious has been thrown away amongst the rubbish—something which might have been saved.

Since I am dealing with past events, my vocabulary is often antiquated. For instance I call English people "Anglo-Indians." And throughout I use "India" in the old, and as it seems to me the true, sense of the word to designate the whole sub-continent. Much as I sympathise with the present government at New Delhi, I wish it had not chosen "India" to describe its territory. Politicians are too prone to plunder the past.

Besides acknowledging my debt to Sir Malcolm Darling, I should like to thank Mrs. F. E. Barger, Mr. Arthur Cole, Mr. M. V. Desai, Mr. Ian Stephens and Madame van Bierfliet for the help which they have given in various ways.

Cambridge, 1953.

CONTENTS

PLATES

THE ASSEMBLED COURT, 1913

PLAYING JUBBU

HOUSE PARTY MEMENTO

Inscribed by His Highness: "Fine combination of varied
east and cultured west."

Seated left to right: E. M. Forster; His Highness; Malarao Sahib.
Standing: Horse Doctor; Deolekr Sahib.

His Highness's Private Secretary

Bapu Sahib

PART OF THE COURT, 1921
Front row left to right: the Dewan; Bhau Sahib; His Highness;
the young Prince; Waghalkar Sahib; the Commander in Chief.
Two of His Highness's daughters are behind him.

AFTER A PENITENTIAL FAST
His Highness at Pondicherry, 1934

LETTERS OF 1912-13

Guest House, Dewas Senior
Christmas Day, 1912

I am at Dewas at last. On the 23rd I was in the club at Indore with Major Luard who mentioned my name aloud, when up sprang a bright and tiny young Indian, and wrung me by both hands. This was the Rajah of Dewas.

He had already sent me a charming telegram, saying he was expecting me. I also understood he was sending a carriage for me on the morrow. This, however, didn't arrive, and the Luards, very kind and not surprised, got the Maharajah of Indore's motor. Baldeo and luggage packed in behind, and we whizzed over to Dewas in style—it is twenty-three miles. There I found the Goodalls, Mrs. Darling and son, and another man; Malcolm Darling arrived this morning. The Rajah is away until tomorrow, but the Dewan (Prime Minister) came to greet us and was very pleasant. In the evening we went to the Tennis Club—all Indians—and drove back through the tidy little town.

The Guest House is at the edge of a lake in which my clothes are being washed and Baldeo has been bathing. *I am in a tent—imagine it possible on Xmas Day!—a very superior tent with passage all round the central room, and many doors. The garden, naturally so pretty, is agog with terrible streamers and a crimson triumphal arch with "Welcome to our Xmas Guests" on it, and many flags of George and Mary. We are only here till the first of January, I fear. Dewas is not beautiful, but there is a sacred hill above it, covered with chapels, which makes the scenery interesting.*

I had tea and toast at seven, brought to the tent by Baldeo, and I gave him two rupees as advised, saying "Bara din ke waste" ("For the sake of the great day") and meaning a Xmas box. He replied, "Bahut achha" ("Very good"), and salaamed. There seems to be no Indian word for thank you. Then a procession arrived from the Palace—a man with streamers on a stick led it, and fourteen servants followed, each carrying a large metal plate under an embroidered coverlid. Two plates for each of us: one was divided into four quarters which were filled with candied sugar, monkey nuts, pistachio nuts, and pudding-sultanas respectively; the second plate held fruit and vegetables. All fourteen were laid down with salaams on the verandah, while the Dewan smiled benignly. Then we break-

fasted, he sitting at a little distance from the table.

The Rajah, when he comes, will take his meals with us, and eat anything but beef. Their habits vary very much. There is great fun ahead. Goodall and his wife are to be married again in Indian fashion and ride on the top of an elephant: a native banquet afterwards. Another day there will be players.

Malcolm came direct from Delhi, and was full of the bomb disaster there. I needn't go into details as you will have had only too many in the papers. He thinks it a pity that Lord Hardinge, finding his wound was slight, did not go on from the hospital to the Durbar, for then it would have made a great impression and prevented the seditious party from saying that the Viceroy had never reached Delhi. I expect his nerves were too much shattered, even though he was not hurt. It is a dreadful business—not only in itself, but because it will strengthen the reactionary party. Malcolm says that after the news came, several Englishmen—officials of high position, too—were anxious for the Tommies to be turned to fire at the crowd, and seemed really sorry that the Viceroy had not been killed, because then there would have been *a better excuse for doing such a thing. Malcolm was in the Punjab procession, which preceded the Viceregal one, and heard the news en route. I know the Chandni Chauk: Dr. Ansari's rooms were at the top of it. Mohammedans are in the most frightful state, because Delhi is their city, and the bomb was probably thrown by some Hindu who was angry at the transfer of the capital from Calcutta. No police were at hand, but they are not to be blamed as Hardinge dislikes them and had counterordered them.*

It is appropriate that I should have first seen the Ruler of Dewas at a moment of crisis. When he leapt up to greet me in that Indore club, he was in the midst of composing an enormous telegram of sympathy, congratulation and indignation to the Viceroy on the subject of the Delhi outrage. Almost the last time I saw him—nine years later—he was again composing an enormous telegram. And almost the last time I had news of him—twenty-five years later—he had been composing an enormous telegram, and again to a Viceroy.

In my next letter, I record my first glimpse of his kingdom.

26th December

Unversed though I am in politics, I must really give you some account of this amazing little state, which can have no parallel, except in a Gilbert and Sullivan opera. In the eighteenth century, the then Rajah, being fond of his brother, gave him a share in the government, and his descendants extended the courtesy to his (the brother's) descendants. When the English came (early nineteenth century) they seem to have mistaken the situation, and supposed that there were two independent rulers in the same city. They guaranteed both, with the result that now there are twin dynasties, with their possessions all peppered in and out of each other. Each has his own court, his own army, his own water works and tennis club, his own palace, before each of which different bands play different tunes at the same hour every evening.

It is true that Devi—the sacred mountain that stands above the distracted city like an acropolis—has at last been divided between them, so that each can get to his own shrine without walking on the other's footpath; and it is true that they have come to an arrangement over the flagstaff on the top, by which it belongs to both of them—upper half to one, lower half to the other, and the flag flying half-mast to be neutral.

Our host—Rajah of Dewas, Senior Branch, is his title—was Darling's pupil five years ago, and they are devoted to each other. I have only seen him for a moment, but he struck me as a most charming and able young man. The "Junior Branch," who is older and less competent, we never see.

I am getting the habit of early rising—long may it last!—and was up to see the sun come out of the palm trees this morning, and the cranes go hunting for their breakfast in the lake. The air was delicious, and silent except for little drums that were being beaten in the temples. Devi turned brown-pink above us, and presently the light reached the plain, gilding indiscriminately the motor garage of the Junior Branch and the elephants of the Senior.

One of these elephants we are to ride shortly, amid the applause of the (appropriate) populace, and it is to land us into an Indian banquet, with garlands and speeches and I don't know what. Another day we are to see native acting, but—anxious to catch the mail—I write before these festivities have come off. The Rajah is away for the moment, at a Maratha conference. I hope he will be back this evening, after which, as soon as the priests have purified him from the railway train, he will spend all his time with us.

January 1st [1913]

So many delights that I snatch with difficulty a moment to describe them to you. Garlanded with jasmine and roses, I await the carriage that takes us to the Indian theatre, erected for the Xmas season outside the Old Palace. But to proceed.

December 29th the Rajah gave an Indian banquet to the newly married pair. I have both forgotten the time it was meant to be and the time it was. As usual they differed widely, but at all events, as darkness fell, the garden and road by the Guest House filled up with soldiers, policemen, horses, children, torchbearers, and a most gorgeous elephant. (There are two state elephants but the other did not feel quite well.) Goodall was to wear Indian dress, and I retired to my tent to put on my English evening things.

Baldeo, much excited by the splendour that surrounded us, was making the best of my simple wardrobe and helping to snip my shirt cuffs where they were frayed, when there was a cry of "May I come in?" and enter the Rajah, bearing Indian raiment for me also. A Sirdar (courtier) came with him, a very charming boy,* and they two aided Baldeo to undress me and redress me. It was a very funny scene. At first nothing fitted, but the Rajah sent for other garments off people's backs until I was suited. Let me describe myself. Shoes—I had to take them off when the Palace was reached, so they don't count. My legs were clad in jodhpurs made of white muslin. Hanging outside these was the youthful Sirdar's white shirt, but it was concealed by a waistcoat the colours of a Neapolitan ice—red, white and green, and this was almost concealed by my chief garment—a magnificent coat of claret-coloured silk, trimmed with gold. I never found out to whom this belonged. It came to below my knees and fitted round my wrists closely and very well, and closely to my body. Cocked rakishly over one ear was a Maratha turban of scarlet and gold—not to be confused with the ordinary turban; it is a made-up affair, more like a cocked hat. Nor was this all. I carried in my left hand a scarf of orange-coloured silk with gold ends, and before the evening ended a mark like a loaf of bread was stamped on my forehead in crimson, meaning that I was of the sect of Shiva.

* Waghalkar Sahib: I met and liked him again in later years.

Meanwhile, the others too had been surprised with Indian costumes, Malcolm looking very fine in pink with a sword, and the other man in purple. The ladies went as themselves. At last we were ready, and really it was a glorious sight when the Goodalls were perched on the elephant, sitting on real cloth of gold, with torches around them, and above, splendid starlight. The band played, the children cheered, and the Darlings' nice old Ayah stood in the verandah invoking blessings from Heaven. We went each in a carriage with Sirdars: I had two old men and one fat one, all gorgeous, but conversation not as good as our clothes. An elephant being pensive in its walk, we didn't reach the New Palace for a long time, though it is close to the Guest House. Hideous building! But it was too dark to see it. After the Rajah had welcomed us we went to the banquet room. This again I must try to describe to you.

We all sat on the floor, cross-legged, round the edge of a great hall, the servants running about in the middle. Each was on a legless chair and had in front a tray like a bed tray on which was a metal tray, on which the foods were ranged. The Brahmins ate no meat, and were waited on by special attendants, naked to the waist. The rest of us had meat as well as the other dishes. Round each man's little domain an ornamental pattern was stencilled in chalk on the floor. My tray was arranged somewhat as follows, but "Jane, Jane, however shall we recollect the dishes?" as Miss Bates remarked.

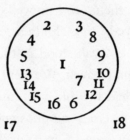

1. A mound of delicious rice—a great stand-by.
2. Brown tennis balls of sugar—not bad.
3. Golden curlicues—sweet to sickliness.
4. Little spicy rissoles.
5. Second mound of rice, mixed with spices and lentils.
6. Third mound of rice, full of sugar and sultanas—very nice.
7. Curry in metal dish—to be mixed with rice No. 1.
8. Sauce, as if made from apples that felt poorly. Also to be mixed with rice, but only once by me.

9. Another sauce, chooey-booey and brown.

10, 11, 12. Three dreadful little dishes that tasted of nothing till they were well in your mouth, when your whole tongue suddenly burst into flame. I got to hate this side of the tray.

13. Long thin cake, like a brandy snap but salt.

14. It may have been vermicelli.

15. As for canaries.

16. Fourth mound of rice to which I never came.

17. Water.

18. Native bread—thin oat-cake type.

Some of these dishes had been cooked on the supposition that an elephant arrives punctually, and lay cooling on our trays when we joined them. Others were brought round hot by the servants who took a fistful and laid it down wherever there was room. Sometimes this was difficult, and the elder dishes had to be rearranged, and accommodate themselves. When my sweet rice arrived, a great pushing and squeezing and patting took place, which I rather resented, not knowing how attached I should become to the newcomer. Everything had to be eaten with the hand, and with one hand—it is bad manners to use the left—and I was in terror of spoiling my borrowed plumes. Much fell, but mostly into the napkin, and the handkerchief that I had brought with me. I also feared to kneel in the sauces or to trail my orange scarf in the ornamental chalk border, which came off at the slightest touch and actually did get onto the jodhpurs. The cramp, too, was now and then awful. The courtiers saw that I was in pain, and told the servants to move the tray that I might stretch, but I refused, nor would I touch the entire English dinner that was handed round during the meal—roast chicken, vegetables, blancmange, etc.

As each guest finished, he sang a little song from the Vedas in praise of some god, and the Rajah was, as usual, charming. He made the Goodalls feed each other five times and pronounce each other's name aloud. These are among their marriage customs. Afterwards he, his brother, the Dewan, and all of us went onto the palace roof, where was champagne and betel nut, and we danced in our grand clothes and our socks to the music of the band which was playing down in the square. This suited me very well.

We were interrupted by a message from the Rani—she desired to see us. This was a great surprise to me.

The two ladies went first, and then we, and had a lovely vision. She was extraordinarily beautiful, with dark "gazelle" eyes. Having shaken hands all round, she leant against the doorpost and said nothing. There was an awkward, if respectful, pause, and after Malcolm had talked a little Urdu and received no answer, we went. Her dress was on the negligee side, but she had not been intending to receive. The Rajah was pleased she had sent for us. He longs to modernise her, but she remains a lovely wild creature.

We returned to the hall below, sitting on the floor again and hearing a little singing from nautch girls. We drove back to the Guest House to find Mrs. Darling and Mrs. Goodall in the most magnificent Indian dresses: the Rani had dressed them and sent them back in a purdah carriage.—So ended a very charming evening, full of splendour yet free of formality.

The 30th brought festivities of a very different kind. The Agent to the Governor General, who lives at Indore, and his subordinate the Political Agent from Neemuch, each brought a party, and we all had lunch here, very stiff and straight, the Rajah being quite another person. It is odd that I should have seen so much of the side of life that is hidden from most English people. As at Chhatarpur, I became privy to all the anxieties through which an Indian passes when his political superiors call. Would all go well, what would they think of him, etc.? Oh dear, why would the servants not bring lunch: would I run and hurry them up, etc.?

All went well. The A.G.G. was a very fine fellow; his wife not nice. The P.A., who planted himself on the state for the night and used and broke all the motors, was not nice either, but on the other hand he brought three Italian guests with him who were. As their English was of the feeblest, I figured. We had an acrobatic performance after tea in the Guest House garden, and Indian theatre in the evening—tawdry and dull. We applauded one act out of politeness and they did it all again. As soon as the guests had gone, the Rajah sported like a kitten.

The chief event of January 1st was the Durbar in the Old Palace—rather a beautiful building in the heart of the town. Dressed in white, he sat on the "Gaddi"—half bed, half throne—leaning against a white bolster with peacock fans waving over his head. The court sat cross-legged all down the room on each

side, we in an alcove on chairs: he would not have us
squatting. All offered "nazzir" (homage) which he re-
mitted to the servants. His expression changed as each
came up: to the Sirdars he was dignified, to the
Maratha guests courteous and warm: he laughed behind his hand when the Subedhar, his buffoon, came.
(This is a puzzling unattractive man; a spy from
Kolhapur I am told. H.H.* is always translating his
droll speeches and I can't see their drollery: sometimes
his turban is set on fire, which makes me wretched.
He takes care of Lady, the flea-bitten little dog.)

After each had paid homage, the Rajah made a long
dull speech about the constitutional changes that he
is making—a new advisory council; I believe it is important. No one was much pleased. Then scent and
betel nut were distributed all round. The proceedings
lasted two hours, and were impressive owing to the
architecture of the fine little hall and to the dresses.
But oh the pictures! The dear creature has not a
glimmer of taste and on the dark wooden pillars are
hung "Love me, love my dog," or Xmas plates from
the Graphic. Even when the subjects are Hindu they

* His Highness. This abbreviation is used throughout the book
in referring to the Maharajah.

are cheap prints, and he has actually put glass balls to swing from the ceiling. My heart aches, for he is an active and able ruler, and if he lives long, Dewas will look like the Euston Road. Malcolm has asked him to take the balls away, and he will do so, but it's no good. Malcolm and Josie chose all the decorations for the New Palace, but the tints couldn't "quite be matched," and the result is a nightmare of sickly green, proudly shown as an example of English taste. The Maharajah of Chhatarpur, on the other hand, seemed incapable of doing anything which wasn't beautiful.

Next day, my visit ended. It had only lasted a week, but had given me glimpses of what was to become familiar later. There are a few notes about it in my diary. I record how I walked up Devi before breakfast, also how I saw, down in the plain, a grave of earth under a peepul tree, polished roots forming its precincts. A garland of jasmine hung on the head of the grave, sticks of burning cotton wool soaked in incense were stuck in its sides, a heap of grain with divine cooking utensils lay in front. A man in a red turban told us that he was a clerk who wanted eight rupees per month instead of seven, and he came here to pray for this raise every Thursday. An old woman was there too: she kept the grave clean, for which a piece of land was settled on her. "A shrine of Durga," Malcolm thought, but he was wrong, it was Moslem; one was always going to be wrong.

On the final afternoon we played that typically British game, "Characters," at the edge of a little tank. The Rajah wanted to mark all our characters as high as possible provided Malcolm came out highest, but was puzzled because one of the qualities for which one could be marked was passion. "Is not passion bad?" he enquired anxiously.

Then we lunched—"but not too near those red stones, Malcolm, I had rather not." His clever merry little face peeped out of a huge turban: he was charming, he was lovable, it was impossible to resist him or India.

All the same, I find a stern little entry: "Land of petty treacheries, of reptiles moving about too cautious to strike each other. No line between the insolent and the servile in social intercourse. In every remark and gesture does not the Indian prince either decrease his own *izzat* or that of his interlocutor? Is there ever civility with manliness here? And is foreign conquest or national character to blame?"

We struck camp on the evening of January 2nd.
The whole court was at the New Palace to bid us
farewell. Transport broke down as before; the Maharajah of Indore again lent his car and the train waited
forty minutes for us at Rutlam. I continued my tour—
I was touristing—and I did not expect to see my delightful host again.

But by good luck our paths crossed at Delhi a
couple of months later.

Delhi
March 6th

*I must relate exciting developments. I am stopping
here with the beloved Rajah of Dewas. He, the Rani,
his brother, the Dewan, and sixty-five attendants have
come to attend a Chiefs' Conference, and my day in
Delhi, which I have now made two, catches them. I
heard through the Darlings of his whereabouts, and
wired; he replied that I should be met at the station.
This, however, did not happen, but Rashid, with
whom I had also been in touch, was there, and after
breakfast we hunted the court out in a tonga: two
trains arrived the same time and they had met the
wrong one.*

The Rajah had taken a room for me at a hotel, but on seeing me exclaimed I must be nearer, and here I am in a delightful upper room, while the courtiers seethe below and the Rajah and his brother are having a bath in the verandah. Sometime we are to have a meal, but when or of what is uncertain, nor is it certain when the Rajah will leave Delhi, nor whether for Lahore to stop with the Darlings or for Hardwar to bathe in the sacred river there. He was so sweet when I arrived—darted up from behind and put his hands over my eyes. Dewan Sahib was also pleasant, and they have taught the son and heir to scream less at Europeans and, with an agonised expression, to shake hands. He is such a beautiful child. The Rani, and many handmaidens, sit crouched in a dense mass behind a screen all the time.

I think I must go now. I hope to add more before evening. . . .

No, I needn't go. The Rajah is doing pujah after his bath, streams of water from which are flowing over the garden. My meal is coming from the hotel, as it is a fast day in honour of Shiva and the court are on a diet of potatoes and sweets. I really don't know what happens next—one so seldom does.

It is now an hour since the embassy started to bring food from the hotel. Dewan Sahib suggests biscuits and sweets to go on with, but these too have foundered. My room has pictures of Krishna on the walls, interspersed with the Archbishop of Canterbury crowning the King and Queen in Westminster Abbey. And now the light refreshments come—saucers of sultanas and monkey nuts, pastry knobs, cardamum, sweets, cold potatoes and Marie biscuits, grouped round a cup of hot spiced milk.

The next letter, of the same date, dives a little deeper. It is written to my old friend Mrs. Aylward, who was profoundly Christian and was furthermore interested in all manifestations of religion.

Delhi

March 6th, 1913

The Rajah has just been talking to me, cross-legged and barefoot on a little cane chair. We had a long talk about religion, during which I often thought of you. Indians are so easy and communicative on this subject, whereas English people are mostly offended when it is introduced, or else shocked if there is a difference of opinion. His attitude was very difficult for a Westerner. *He believes that we—men, birds, everything—are part of God, and that men have developed more than birds because they have come nearer to realising this.*

That isn't so difficult; but when I asked why we had any of us ever been severed from God, he explained it by God becoming unconscious that we were parts of him, owing to his energy at some time being concentrated elsewhere. "So," *he said,* "a man who is thinking of something else may become unconscious of the existence of his own hand for a time, and feel nothing when it is touched." *Salvation, then, is the thrill which we feel when God again becomes conscious of us, and all our life we must train our perceptions so that we may be capable of feeling when the time comes.*

I think I see what lies at the back of this—if you believe that the universe was God's conscious creation, you are faced with the fact that he has consciously created suffering and sin, and this the Indian refuses to believe. "We were either put here intentionally or unintentionally," *said the Rajah,* "and it raises fewer difficulties if we suppose it was unintentionally."

4 5

I expect that as I have tried to describe it to you, this reads more like philosophy than religion, but it is inspired by his belief in a being who, though omnipresent, is personal, and whom he calls Krishna. He is really a remarkable man, for all this goes with much practical ability and a sense of humour. In the middle of a chat he will suddenly pray, tapping his forehead and bobbing on his knees, and then continuing the sentence where he left it off; "On days when one feels gratitude, it is well to show it," he said. Today is a great fast day in honour of Shiva, so I have seen a great deal of this, and it has also prevented him eating with me, as he would otherwise have done.

The conversation above described was the first of any importance that we had had. It ended abruptly, for news arrived that the Rani was ill. The Rajah leapt up and round the room, doing pujah to the pictures of Krishna, and said he would return, but did not.

About a month earlier, I had had a Krishna conversation with another ruling prince: the fantastic and poetical Maharajah of Chhatarpur. It took place not in a dull Delhi room, but amidst the magnificent scenery of Bundelkhand. We sat in a palace courtyard on a spur of the wooded Vindhyas with a view over jungle and hills: to the right, the course of the river Ken was marked by darker trees. I asked him whether he meditated.

"Yes—when I can for two hours, and when I am busy for forty-five minutes."

"And can you concentrate and forget your troubles?"

"Oh no, not at all, they come in with me always unless I can meditate on love, for love is the only power that can keep thought out. I try to meditate on Krishna. I do not know that he is a God, but I love Love and Beauty and Wisdom, and I find them in his history. I worship and adore him as a man. If he is divine he will notice me for it and reward me; if he is not, I shall become grass and dust like the others."

While we conversed, a beautiful scarlet bird, twice the size of a swallow, flew near us and distracted the Maharajah of Chhatarpur's thoughts. "Can that be the robin-redbreast?" he enquired. "It glitters like a jewel."

He was nonsensical and elusive, and his fellow potentate of Dewas thought ill of him. But their differ-

47

ent temperaments converged in the adoration of Krishna, and they have between them helped to illuminate Indian religion for me. Later on I shall return to the Maharajah of Chhatarpur.

I left Delhi on March 9th; the following letter was written after my departure.

On the last day at Delhi the Rajah paid some official calls, and I drove round with him but did not go in, remaining in the carriage with Lady, the elderly pug, who goes everywhere, I can't make out why. We ended up at the Cotes', whose acquaintance, as friends of Malcolm's, he wished to make, and then, like a boy loose from school, he grew mad with joy that his duties were over, and bounced up and down among the cushions.

We drove into the city, and came across his brother and various members of the court who had been shopping. Much excitement, and we drove on, but no sooner had we gone twenty yards than he thought it would be fun to have them all with us. But they had got into the electric tram to have the experience, which was new to them, and we followed madly in their wake, blocked by buffaloes and camels and goats

and cows and sweetmeat sellers and pariah dogs. The
tram was disappearing, but the coachman, at the
Rajah's orders, leapt from the box and pursued it on
foot, shouting. After five minutes he came back, leading the whole procession, who got in, together with
their purchases of briar pipes, tobacco, mechanical
monkeys for the children, writing paper, ink, paper
parcels of every size and shape.

In all we were ten—the horses were strong and
went slowly—it looked like a car in a carnival. I sat
between the Rajah, in a huge pale-yellow turban, and
his brother, whose turban was purple and who was
trying to smoke his English pipe. Opposite were the
doctor in red Maratha headdress, a secretary who wore
an orange cup and saucer, and the court buffoon and
spy, on whose knees Lady lay, indifferent to everything. Coachman, another attendant, and footman
made three on the box, while the groom hung on
behind. We attracted, as far as I could make out, no
attention at all, though they all talked louder and
louder, as Indians do when they are happy.

We got back to the royal lodgings at about 7 P.M.,
when a scene of still greater confusion followed. I
wanted to make my own arrangements for getting to

the station, which thanks to Baldeo always work without the slightest hitch—I've only to name the train, and when I arrive five minutes before it goes there he is with all the luggage in the carriage and the bed made if it is a night journey. But no—I was the Rajah's guest and he would arrange—two tongas for the luggage, and he and I alone in a phaeton, while the court, who were going to bathe in the Ganges at Hardwar, should follow behind—the Hardwar train left two hours after mine for Jaipur. But the court had got under way and out of hand, and no sooner did a carriage drive up than they and their dogs and their parrots and their menservants and their maid-servants leapt into it and were off before Baldeo could get the luggage down. Nor could he find anyone to carry it. Nor did the Rajah lose the extra opportunity for confusion which was presented by two entrances to the garden, sending Baldeo to one while a carriage waited at another. At last all grew deathly quiet— everyone had gone but ourselves and the Rani, who was dressing, helped by a handmaiden. Taking Baldeo aside, I said, "Let us not trouble His Highness any more: make any arrangement that you can." The story should end with him doing this, but just then a decrepit band-gharri (four-wheeler) came up, into which I and the luggage got: not the Rajah, who had to stay behind to start the Rani, there being no one left to do this.

It's so typical of the Oriental, who makes a howling mess over one thing and does another with perfect success and grace, that when I reached Delhi station an official met me with railway tickets for myself and Baldeo to Jaipur: the Rajah had ordered them. It is a usual if overwhelming courtesy in the East to do this, and a deadly insult to refuse: and indeed I was pleased to be given tickets by anyone whom I like as much and who is as rich as this man (but I have found it trying when an obscure Indian, whom I didn't care for, once bought my ticket for me—fortunately only to the tune of ninepence).

The tickets—mine first class as against my usual second—did not bring their full joys, for, as it was late, the train had filled up and I could only get an upper berth, and Baldeo no seat at all. The court, entangled with other courts who were also leaving after the Chiefs' Conference, ran up and down the platforms looking for trains. Rashid came too very kindly to see me off, and on top of him the Rajah, *having landed the Rani safely. Off my train went before I was in it—hand-shakings, messages, cries. I caught it up, and proposed to take Baldeo, whom the guard could get in nowhere, into the carriage, but my ass of a fellow traveller protested, and proposed that Baldeo and his own servant—we were in the same plight—should travel on the footboard at the end of the carriage—they were Continental shape—facing full all night to the wind. He said "It would not do, they would not understand"—that argument so dear to fools. Technically he was right, so I could only point out how inconvenient he would find it if his servant fell onto the rails in the night or got ill. At the next station—fifteen minutes on—I prepared to hunt for the guard again, but by now he had come to his senses, and remarked that it did seem rather cold, and that if I was willing to abandon the conventions, he was. So the servants slept on the carriage floor and, whether or not they understood, arrived at Jaipur without pneumonia. The man, I discovered, was an American. Cheers for democracy! He seemed absolutely English —upper-class, Oxford manner—and had evidently moved in high circles at Delhi, dining with the Viceroy and the chiefs according to his own account.*

THE STATE AND ITS RULER

≈§ 1 §≈

"The curious twin States of Dewas," as an old gazetteer well calls them, lie in the middle of India on a
plateau 2,000 feet above the sea. At the time I knew
them, their territories were inextricably mixed with
each other and with the territories of surrounding
states. The administrative confusion must have been
even greater than normal, the Government of India
got periodically puzzled, and the two rulers made
halfhearted attempts to escape each other's embraces.
It was too difficult. They never succeeded. A map of
their possessions lies before me. The Senior Branch
(tinted green) owned 446 square miles, and had a
population of 80,000, the Junior Branch (pink) was
a little smaller. The district of Sarangpur (yellow) was
administered jointly—I know not how, though on one
occasion I took away a carful of rupees from it. The
whole area was divided between the two states not
by towns or sections, but by fields and streets: In
Dewas City, S.B. would own one side of a street and
J.B. the other. The arrangement must have been

unique, and an authoritative English lady, who knew India inside out, once told me that it did not and could not exist, and left me with the feeling that I had never been there.

I first heard of it from Malcolm Darling. In May, 1907, just after he had arrived to take up his duties as tutor and guardian to the young prince, he wrote of "the oddest corner of the world outside Alice in Wonderland," where the two rulers each had his own palace and court and army and national anthem. The army of Dewas Senior then consisted of "80 cavalry, 70 foot and 60 irregulars, also 14 guns; 2 of them are sometimes fired. In the evening the band plays. It numbers at least ten and is therefore an important part of the national forces." Education, being less important, was then joint: each ruler appointed a headmaster who claimed to be in sole charge. The coats of arms were almost identical. Each displayed the Monkey God holding a mountain and supported by elephants and pellets, signifying world dominion, and bore the motto "Two Branches grace one Stem."

Why and when did the branches divide? The family—Ponwar or Puar by name—was Maratha and came north from the Deccan at the end of the seventeenth century in the general Maratha expansion. In the eighteenth century two brothers, Tukoji and Jiwaji, acquired various possessions, including the Dewas area, together with permission from the Peshwa "to carry a banner and sound a drum." They ruled their territory jointly at first, then found division convenient, and initiated the Senior and Junior Branches respectively. It cannot have seemed strange in those days, when organisation was loose and centralisation impossible. It was a family arrangement between two landowners who happened to be royal. And it did not seem strange to the English when they appeared on the scene: on the 12th of December, 1818, a treaty of friendship, signed between the two rulers and the Honourable East India Company, confirmed them respectively in their possessions.

There were several Maratha states. The chief was Kolhapur, some hundreds of miles to the south, in the Deccan. It figures largely in my story. I have never been to Kolhapur but have heard much about it; conservative, proud, subtle, scenically magnificent. Surrounding Dewas were the three important states of Baroda, Gwalior, and Indore. They too come into the story, but in terms of power rather than of prestige, being parvenus. Then there was Dhar (where once I took refuge), a small state closely related dynastically, and there were the Bhonsla rajahs who owned no territory and lived in British India. The whole agglomeration meant much to the ruler of Dewas Senior, especially in his earlier years. He dreamt of fusing it into a Maratha confederacy, perhaps with himself as leader, and, as far as birth and intelligence went, he was well qualified to lead.

Little is clear-cut in India and, having emphasised that the family was Maratha, I must now state that it was Rajput. They claimed—at least our friend did —to represent Rajputs who had ruled in the district as far back as the ninth century. These Rajputs, he declared, had been driven south by hostile Moslems, they had reached the Maratha homeland and had been kindly received there, they had intermarried, he was descended from them, so that in coming northward he was really returning to his own. The claim is not convincing, but it was one of the sources of his pride and I have once or twice put my foot in it by forgetting that he was part of the military mediaeval aristocracy of India, and sprung, at a pinch, from the sun. Practically, and sentimentally, he was Maratha, he looked it, he would at times gaily refer to himself as a Maratha rat, and to Rajputs as stupid warriors: "Fine straightforward chaps. Oh yes, that is what the Government wants a chief to be. A fine chap like a Rajput who notices nothing. Well, I must try." He might have been even more of a Rajput if the leading Rajput prince, the Maharana of Udaipur, had not once snubbed him and sent only a second-class noble to meet him at Udaipur railway station.

Viewed through the cool eyes of British administration, the twin states formed part of the Central India Agency. Too unimportant to have an official specially accredited to them, they were in a group with others under a Political Agent who lived elsewhere. Over the P.A. was the Agent to the Governor General, who lived in the Residency at Indore. Over the A.G.G. was the Political Secretary, living at Delhi or Simla according to the weather. Over him was the Viceroy. Over him the King-Emperor. Dewas and King-Emperor! In Dewas it often seemed that they might have much in common. Could one but short-circuit, all might yet be well.

Viewed through the still cooler eyes of the present

Republic of India, the twin states have entirely disappeared. They are merged in Madhya Bharat, whose capital is Gwalior in hot weather and Indore in cold.

⌘ 2 ⌘

The Ruler was born on January 1st, 1888, so he was exactly nine years younger than myself, though sometimes he seemed much younger and at other times far older and infinitely wiser. He succeeded his uncle, who died childless in 1899 and had intended to adopt him. The adoption was confirmed by his aunt, who lived on into my time, and was then known as the Dowager Maharani. I used to enjoy her company and she contributed much to local colour, but by no means did she hit it off with her nephew, as events will show.

He had a younger brother, called by his friends "Bhau Sahib," and I shall thus refer to him. Bhau Sahib is alive and well, I rejoice to say, and still lives at Dewas; they were devoted to each other and they grew up as boys in the ancestral village of Supa in the Deccan. A happy childhood, like most Indian childhoods; he could recall his father reciting in Marathi the ballads and epics of their race, for hours on end,

and inspiring him with noble thoughts; he could remember searching for family treasure and being de-
terred by a snake. To his mother (she came from
Baroda) he was devoted. Years after her death he still
mourned her, and one day he lamented to me, while
tying a turban, that he no longer took pleasure in
tying it, now that the beloved voice which could
praise his skill had gone. "It is only for the sake of
those who love us that we do things." A dangerous
creed. And there was even danger in his soft domes-
ticated childhood: he grew up in the midst of intrigues. Intrigue became a special subject for him, as
it cannot for an English boy—his voice altered when
he mentioned it. There was endless gossip, there were
exhausting squabbles, particularly between his mother
and his aunt, there were all the grievances of the
zenana over jewelry and precedence, connecting with
the grievances of males outside, there were marriage
connections with other courts, fertile in further grievances and, hidden in this vast domestic hotbed, there
was always the possibility of poison. I know of no
case at Dewas either of poisoning or of attempted
poisoning. But I can recall no less than three poison-
scares. They produced an atmosphere unfamiliar to

the Protestant and pharmaceutical north, and they have to be accepted as part of his emotional heritage.

Before adoption he was known as Bapu Sahib, and that is the name by which he asked me to call him. His close intimates, the Darlings, called him Tukoji or Tukky. His title as ruler was Sir Tukoji Rao III. The Government of India gave him full powers in 1908, the K.C.I.E. in 1911, and the rank of Maharajah a few years later.

His early years were full of promise. He did brilliantly at college, first at Indore and then at Ajmere. When he was eighteen—a slip of a boy with a heavy moustache—a most important event occurred. The Government of India appointed Malcolm Darling, I.C.S., to be his tutor and guardian, and the great friendship of his life began.*

It began doubtfully. He was sensitive, high-spirited and suspicious, and Malcolm, who had never met anyone like him either at Eton or at King's College,

* Although Darling's personal connection with Dewas was continuous, most of his career lay in the Punjab. Three of his books, *The Punjab Peasant, Wisdom and Waste, Rusticus Loquitur*, deal with rural conditions there. His last, and perhaps most fascinating book, *At Freedom's Gate*, describes a ride from Peshawar to the Nerbudda, after the British withdrawal.

Cambridge, did not know how to handle him. The very first week there was a hitch. He did not want to call on his disingenuous aunt. His new tutor ordered him to go. He went, but his eyes flashed fire.

Fortunately Malcolm's mother arrived, and she did much to ease the situation. Warm of heart and simple of spirit, Mrs. Darling soon became friends with the charming Oriental. He drove her out of an evening in his tum-tum. At first he thought she had been set to spy on him, so he tried to trap her.

Having imparted some trifling secrets, he said, "You will not tell any one about this, will you?"

She replied, "No, but I may tell my son, mayn't I?"

If she had merely said "No," he would have continued to mistrust her. As it was, he knew that she was "frank." Their drives rapidly became intimate. They discussed religion as a rule, but on one occasion the conversation took a more delicate turn.

"That is the house where my father's mistress lived; he built it for her," he remarked, pointing to a building casually. Mrs. Darling's principles were strict, and she felt that she must not let this pass.

"But you would not do such a thing," she said, to

which he replied, "Oh no!" but in an unsatisfactory tone of voice; too self-confident.

"We have a text: He that thinketh he standeth, let him take heed lest he fall," said Mrs. Darling gently. He approved of the text and continued: "You remember that old man whose hat you admired last night? He has a mistress."

"But do all the others do it too?" the worried lady gasped, for there had been a large native banquet at which she had enjoyed herself.

Once again the answer was not quite satisfactory: "Oh no—they are more up to date." On this equivocal note they concluded. But they were friends, and the way lay open for the friendship with Malcolm.

Malcolm's letters home give a day-to-day picture of life at Dewas in 1907-08. Besides writing to his family, he corresponded at length with our friend Arthur Cole, and also with myself. It is interesting to see how the place transformed him. When he arrived, he had the feeling of racial superiority which was usual among Englishmen at the time. In a few months he lost it, and it never returned. They became fond of each other and every difficulty vanished: no trouble in visiting her Dowager Highness now.

Affection, all through his chequered life, was the only force to which Bapu Sahib responded. It did not always work, but without it nothing worked. Affection and its attendants of human warmth and instinctive courtesy—when they were present his heart awoke and dictated his actions. In their absence he could be shifty and cunning although he was never cruel. Their friendship lasted until his death: the final years clouded it, but they clouded all things, they were an emanation from the grave. In those early years, with the promise of an important public career opening, the young Englishman and the still younger Indian were full of hope and felt themselves to be symbols of their respective countries, and the pledges of a happier political union. They travelled for three months together, all over India and Burma; when they returned, the state presented an address to each of them, and the boys of the Victoria High School burst into song:

> Let us clap and let us sing
> Let us form a merry ring
> God has safe our Master brought
> Home with precious lessons fraught.

They read Aristotle's *Politics* together; Malcolm was interested in modern agricultural methods, so they were installed, though not for long; they became brothers after marriage, their wives, sisters; the mother of the one became the mother of the other; their friends were in common also, and that is why I was received with such an open heart.

Besides Malcolm's letters, there is his confidential report on his pupil, submitted after he had been with him for a year. In language suited to the officials who were to read it, it analyses the Ruler's character: "If he is treated well in the minor matters of life, he will give much in return. . . . He has hitherto in the matter of women kept rigidly 'to the square'; he is generous, enthusiastic, touchy; ambitious to do something for his fellow Marathas and in this he should be encouraged, for despite local patriotisms he remains loyal to the British and appreciates what they have done." The report also indicates that he is affianced to the daughter of the Maharajah of Kolhapur; she it was whom I was to see, poorly dressed, in my 1912 visit, and that is the only time I have seen her. His feud with the Deccani Brahmins is also touched on; it was his aim to be recognised as a

Kschatriya and to be invested with the Sacred Thread. Thanks to his adroitness, he succeeded; the Brahmins never became important in the court, and the notable religious ceremonies it evolved were not priest-ridden but ruler-ridden. The report ends by putting on record "my sense of the high privilege it has been to be so intimately connected with one whose friendship was so well worth winning."

And then there are the letters which he himself wrote Malcolm after the tutorship ended—particularly in the years 1908-10. This is a unique correspondence, wordy, sprawling, intimate, and giving a moving picture of his youthful hopes, his nobility, unselfishness, introspectiveness:

I want my letters to you to be absolutely genuine. I mean letters written as I think in my mind at once. When there is another person like a clerk sitting near one, one always ponders a little and then dictates so as to avoid mistakes, etc. Then I think the letter is not quite genuine, though the thoughts are, but words and style are not.

Genuineness is achieved. What other prince, in India or elsewhere, could have written as follows?

Somehow or other I feel I am not suited at all to be of any use or help to anybody in the world and I feel that circumstances keep me alone without my real relatives like yourself, mother and wife. What I have begun nowadays to feel is that to be a ruler is to be left alone by all friends and relatives. In my case Almighty has been working like that I cannot understand it. Sometimes I feel that if I am fated to be alone then the world is not worth living. I cannot really understand why all these thoughts come to me nowadays, and I am quite depressed in mind, though I try to hide the feelings, and to keep busy.

He did keep busy. One side of him was versatile and resourceful. He could make a Durbar speech on the foundation of a girls' school, and include enlightened remarks like this:

It is the naturally weak that most require protection. And the greatest protection of all is the protection of an enlightened mind. . . . One may sympathise instinctively with those who talk of race and nationality, but civilisation, which they often forget, is greater than these.

Or again:

The germs of the present unrest in India were laid by that benefactor of the human race, education.

The Kolhapur wedding took place in March, 1908, the union being consummated six months later. Malcolm and his sisters went to the wedding, and he has recorded it; the arrival at Kolhapur railway station: the giant Maharajah of Kolhapur in pale green silk with a sash of gold round his huge waist: the meeting of the two potentates: the band from Dewas playing "Oft in danger, oft in woe," in new red and green uniforms: elephants with silver howdahs and trappings of gold, two of them dragging a sort of railway saloon into which the Dewas ladies were pushed: the bridegroom perched high on the roof of the saloon —it was fenced with a golden rail to prevent him falling off. Slowly they advanced and swiftly the ladies quarrelled. His aunt was as always jealous and awkward and tried to separate him from his mother whom she accused of having "unlucky feet"—*i.e.*, the evil eye: a bitter feud sprang up in his sumptuous camp which he had to pacify. Then there were disobliging rumours, set about by the local Brahmins: the wedding hall was to collapse, the bride was to die as a sacrifice against plague and famine, the bridegroom was to go mad and so on and so forth. Danger was in fact nearer than they realised. A bomb had been despatched by seditionists from Poonah which was to be hurled into the wedding enclosure and destroy them all. It arrived too late.*

Always susceptible to women, he was deeply in love, and his letters reveal his emotions and his joy and pride at the splendid alliance. Personally and dynastically everything was perfect: moreover the bride was most beautiful, though to this in his delicacy he does not refer. Later in the year, when he came to fetch her away from Kolhapur, there was a pathetic and rather ominous scene. She was devoted to hunting, and her father had organised a great final shikar for her, in which her husband took part, although no sportsman. At first all went merrily "and I thought I am very lucky in respect of getting a very good-natured and affectionate wife." But towards the end a spasm of grief convulsed the company: "His Highness with all the shikar party and also the ladies were practically doing nothing but either weeping or sobbing

* See Chirol, *Indian Unrest.*

with the idea of my wife's departure from Kolhapur. She is wonderfully popular, and she, poor girl, could not help feeling the separation of her native land and the people who brought her up and played with her in childhood." It was as if she was leaving her heart behind. Her parents were too upset to see her off at the station, and only a few attendants accompanied her into exile, out of courtesy to the husband whose orders she would henceforward obey.

On November the 19th, 1908, at 5:30, the handsome young couple entered Dewas upon an elephant, "she in the back part with curtains." A second elephant followed with Bhau Sahib on it. Everyone else walked with the exception of "our tall and humorous Senapati" (commander in chief), who was on a horse. The decorations were profuse, the loyal mottoes on the arches were so numerous that he had not the time to read them; the court of Dewas Junior had also deployed; they entered the Old Palace for an hour to worship at the dynastic shrine, stayed for a moment at the house of his dead mother (she had died since the spring) and reached the New Palace at 9:30.

There the wild little girl took up her residence, in a comparatively obscure state, with a husband for whom nothing in her upbringing had prepared her, and whose altruism must have been puzzling. The letters breathe unqualified rapture: he has been never so happy: may he succeed in making his wife happy! Then he gets anxious about her health: she has had fever, hysteria, she must go back for a change to Kolhapur. Then there is a confused and troubled letter (sixteen full sheets) about two of her maid-servants, Parvati and Radha. They are at loggerheads, and Parvati goes to her mistress and accuses Radha of having had intercourse with him. He swears his innocence, and we readily believe him, but his wife, incapable of examining evidence, flies into a rage and beats Radha. He remonstrates with her, she refuses to see him, and again she falls ill.

There for the moment the Kolhapur alliance must be left.

Malcolm had also married—a union which was to bring happiness and help to others as well as to him-self. Josie shared his devotion to India and, having fewer obligations, could display the unstinted warmth that India appreciates. No one less like a mem-sahib can be imagined; unconventional, ardent, fearless, she fitted indifferently into official circles at Lahore and elsewhere, indeed sometimes she did not fit in at all.

Dewas at once became her spiritual home. Intuitively she understood "Tukoji" and his approach to life; she loved not only him but his people and she was instantly beloved by them. Her counsel and sympathy were to mean much to him in the coming years, and her death (she died in 1932) may have accelerated the final collapse.

<§ 3 §>

I have tried to outline our friend's problems and his character. He was certainly a genius and possibly a saint, and he had to be a king. Now comes the easier task of indicating the outward scene where his drama was to be played. Let me briefly locate the New Palace, the Old Palace, the Guest House and Devi.

The New Palace was a-building during both my visits, and what an a-building that was! Founded in honour of his father, it was officially known as the Shri Anand Bhuvan Palace; it was shoddy, ignoble, colourless—a yellow-white impression prevails. It did its best to surround a courtyard, where my happier memories centre, for here sometimes a carpet would be spread and we would sit on it in a great semicircle, with glasses of port and whisky by our sides, and play an excellent card game called Jubbu. This was charming—all so gay and mischievous and the Ruler the ringleader.

Behind us rose the ugly Durbar Hall, above that the state drawing room, and round the other sides were rooms both finished and unfinished and of assorted sizes. It was often difficult to know which room one was in, for not one was either holy or homely. Hygienically the New Palace was well placed, right away from the town. It stood in a compound as featureless as itself, Bhau Sahib's residence standing near it. Outside ran the road to Indore, edged with unimpressive trees. On all sides the light fell blankly. Here, indeed, was a very dull India, except for Devi, the sacred acropolis with the rakish cap, half a mile away.

The Old Palace was in every way a contrast. Built in the eighteenth century, it huddled in the middle of the city. It was inconvenient, dirty, dark, and a hotbed of intrigue: "Intrigue has started in the Old Palace again, *I will* not have it," H.H. would occasionally exclaim. Here lurked the proud ancestral servants, some of them ancestral by-blows. But here too, opening along one side of the courtyard, was the dynastic shrine, and above it lay the Durbar Hall with the sacred bed by which a lamp always burned. Here too was the ancient armoury. The place had the quality known as "numinous": it carried one away from the bleak light into another of the Indias, and on the few occasions we slept there I had a feeling of liberation and of initiation. The royal tombs were also mysterious if seen from a boat on the Tank, and in the evening light, and unexpectedly. The Old Palace and the tombs lay in the background of our activities. We would ignore them for weeks but they were always waiting, and I expect they were in his mind when he died.

Round the Guest House no sentiments need cling. It was a dark red dump, dumped by itself by the waters of the Tank when there was any water. When there was no water, it looked over cracked mud and stranded thorn bushes towards the distant town. Here the European visitors and officials stayed or were supposed to stay; here I stayed in 1912, but no one loved the Guest House. It was only a quarter of a mile from the New Palace, and was the excuse for a short walk. Some pleasant gardens were beyond it. Devi again dominated and, when the flood water was out, could look coquettish upside down.

Devi (or Devivasini, the Goddess' Residence) probably gave Dewas its name. It rose about three hundred feet above the level. Stone steps led up to the dark cave of Chamunda on the top. She was a barbaric vermilion object, not often approached by us. Sometimes there were pilgrimages, and at certain festivals she played a part in the ritual. Who was Chamunda, and how long had she resided up there? I never found out, but it was agreed that she had been around longer than anyone else.

She concludes the curiosities of Dewas. Nothing detained the tourist there, and the surrounding domain was equally unspectacular. No antiquities, no picturesque scenery, no large rivers or mountains or forests, no large wild animals, "usual birds and fishes," according to the gazetteer, no factories, no railway station. Only agriculture. Flat or rolling fields, occasionally broken by flat-topped hills. Agriculture, the state's mainstay. Wheat, millet, cotton.

Amidst these surroundings, I was to pass six months of 1921 in the capacity of a Private Secretary.

LETTERS OF 1921

By the time I paid my second visit to Dewas, the Ruler's position had changed, for good and for evil. Politically things were excellent. He had remained loyal to the British and enthusiastically loyal to the King-Emperor, whom he regarded as his feudatory chief, and he had done all he could to assist the Allies during the First World War. Consequently he was highly esteemed in official circles, and Sir Valentine Chirol, a travelling journalist of repute, had signalised him as one of the most enlightened of the younger princes, and had made his name known to a wider public.

On the other hand, there had been an appalling domestic disaster. His marriage had crashed, and in the winter of 1916 he had sent his wife back to Kolhapur. That anyhow was his account: her family asserted that she had fled from him. In either case he, a small prince, had offended a great one, and his fortunes henceforward declined. I have never known the rights of the affair; this way and that way one can hear any-

79

thing one likes in an Indian court. I know that he was devoted to her when they married—his letters remain to prove that—and I also know that he could live affectionately and faithfully with the same woman for years. My conjecture is that she had been alienated from him by a hostile relative. There was one son to the unhappy marriage—Vikramsinha, known to his familiars as Vikky, whom I had seen as a child during my first visit. I did not see him during my second visit, as he was up in the hills. He had been born at Kolhapur, but he grew up under his father's control.

H.H. was so high-spirited, so subtle, and so proud that it was often difficult to know what he felt. He certainly realised that a blow had been struck at Maratha unity, and that he had made an implacable enemy of the leading Maratha power. And he certainly felt lonely. Though a domestic life—and a happy one—was reopening for him, he needed some friend who stood outside the court and its intrigues. He begged Malcolm to be his Private Secretary. Malcolm declined but recommended a Colonel Wilson, about whom there will be much to say in the sequel. Colonel Wilson—an elderly soldier who had done administrative work in India and knew Indian languages and ways—proved a success. In the spring of 1921 he went back to England for a few months' sick leave and it was arranged that I should go to Dewas as a stopgap in his absence.

I was delighted. My fare both ways was to be paid. I was to get three hundred rupees per month. I was not clear what I was to do, nor when I came away was I clear what I had done. But off I went in the highest spirits, and on a P. & O. which was well up to sample: the voyage ended in "feverish gaiety, concerts, juggling with prizes, quarrels between elderly men over a game of deck quoits, special meeting of Sports Committee to adjudicate same"—in fact in all the things I was about to escape. Dewas was not my only objective. I wanted to see Masood, my Moslem friend, who was now Director of Education at Hyderabad.

✑ SETTLING IN ✒

c/o the Goodalls,
Nepean Road,
Bombay
March 28th, 1921

I will begin a letter, now that I see a little light in my plans. I have had a comfortable yet rather annoying arrival. We got in on the 26th. No one to meet me, so I drove from the quay to Cook's and found nothing there at all—nothing from Dewas, nothing from Baldeo, and neither a letter nor money from Masood. I wrote to him twice from England, I wired from Aden: now I have written to him from here and asked him to wire, and still have not heard. The Goodalls have most hospitably received me—otherwise I don't know what I should have done.

However, as I was in the Bombay post office this morning struggling with the situation, two nobles of the Dewas court rushed up to me with cries of joy. They had got Goodall's address but got it wrong— Napier Road for Nepean. We have settled to leave this evening. I must get my clothes at Mhow, and the Dewas servants will look after me until one of my own arrives.

They were very charming and friendly. We went on to see Bhau Sahib, who is a member of the new Council and has a "flat" here. I was asked, "Are the London flats like these?" The ground floor was occupied by an aged man who lay asleep upon a sort of bier with a dirty cloth stretched over him. His naked and rigid feet stuck out.

Then we climbed a shaky wooden staircase on which were piles of mortar, interspersed with food and servants as we neared the top. A fat lady-dog then hove in sight, and I knew we must have reached the flat because, though not the lady-dog I remembered, she had the same tousled turnout. Bhau Sahib and I made conversation while the state motor, which had gone to seek petrol, failed to return. "Someone important" had to be sent after it.

The Secretary, whom I remembered at Delhi (a cheerful intelligent man), drove me back to the Goodalls, and he and Mrs. Goodall had a pleasant chat. He says he will send for my luggage at six. The train goes at nine. I wonder! And when I reach Dewas

I expect that the Maharajah will either have left for
Bombay or will want me at once to return there with
him.

The New Palace,
Dewas Senior *
April 1st, 1921

I arrived Tuesday and still feel rather dazed and
dreamy. All goes well. Masood had been visiting educational establishments for a month on end in the
jungle, where there are no posts, and my letters had
been accumulating. He has sent me masses of money,
but of course I don't need it now. I have repaid
Goodall.

Where to begin? I caught the night train at Bombay, and had not a very comfortable journey. The
Indian trains have gone downhill in the last ten years.
My painted escort (they had been celebrating Holi)
were all that is polite at the junctions, and suffered
me not to put my hand into my pocket, even for a
cup of tea. The last section was through the Vindhya
Hills—very wild and fine. Most of the trees and

* All my subsequent letters are from this address, unless otherwise stated.

vegetation scorched up, but here and there an alarmingly green tree, standing up as if it had been cut out of plasticine. A nice car met me at Indore, and leaving heavy luggage with escort, I sped along the chaussée for twenty-three miles—a dull drive and a dull evening: the road was straight and rough and edged with small dreary trees and we passed a dead cow round which vultures were gathering.

However, at the palace door was His Highness, capering bareheaded, and very charming and friendly. Almost his first question was about you. Then he dictated cables to his Indian secretary: for you and for Malcolm: and after dinner we sped to a party given by the cavalry—I in Indian dress. Fairly simple. White jodhpurs and shirt outside them, coat and waistcoat of silk: and yards and yards of scarlet-crimson stuff wound into a tremendous turban. We were welcomed by the Commander in Chief (whose turban was of hedge-sparrow blue), while his army played their national anthem; and then we had tea and sweets at little tables. Acting and singing followed. I crossed my legs as long as they would bear it, then sat behind on a chair and reflected with pleasure that there was not another European within a radius of twenty miles.

I feel I shall never get through the news. Life here will be queer beyond description. The New Palace ("a memorial to my late father") is still building, and the parts of it that were built ten years ago are already falling down. You would weep at the destruction, expense, and hideousness, and I do almost. We live amongst rubble and mortar, and excavations whence six men carry a basket of earth, no larger than a cat's, twenty yards once in five minutes. I have not yet discovered who loosens the earth, but am familiar with the boy who scrabbles it into the basket with his fingers, the man who bears it on his head along the bottom of the chasm, the next man—very chatty and almost naked—who receives it from him and, merely turning round, places it on the head of No. 4. No. 4 begins the ascent, No. 5 continues it, and No. 6, who is immensely old, totters along the surface and drops the earth onto a heap which will have some day to be cleared away. And the basket has to be passed back. This is the scene under my window, but for acres around the soil is pitted with similar efforts, slabs of marble lie about, roads lead nowhere, costly fruit trees die for want of water, and I have discovered incidentally that £1,000 worth (figure accurate) of electric batteries lie in a room near at hand and will spoil unless fixed promptly.

I can't start now on the inside of the palace—two pianos (one a grand), a harmonium, and a dulciphone, all new and all unplayable, their notes sticking and their frames cracked by the dryness. I look into a room —dozens of warped towel-horses are stabled there, or a new suite of drawing-room chairs with their insides gushing out. I open a cupboard near the bath and find it full of teapots, I ask for a bookcase and it bows when it sees me and lies rattling on the floor. And so on and so forth. I don't know what to do about it all, and scarcely what to feel. It's no good trying to make something different out of it, for it is as profoundly Indian as an Indian temple. I tell H.H. about the worst things, and he is delighted with me, and I wire for a piano-tuner from Bombay, and say that all work must be stopped until the powerhouse is enlarged and the batteries installed. But already I have no illusions. Colonel Wilson really was some good, for he knew all about motorcars, etc., and could speak the language.

The palace is inhabited by four chief people—me, H.H., Malarao Sahib, and Deolekr Sahib—and if there ever was a normal meal we should find ourselves at it. Malarao is of lofty lineage—a sallow young man with a headache on which I have been trying aspirin. I think he is nice, and he's as pleasant as his lack of English permits. He is Mayor of the Palace, and I apply to him when a door won't shut or a drawer closes with the jaws of death on its contents, or I want my bed carried out onto the roof, or if dead flowers are put on the table for a dinner party, or sparrows build in the ceiling. Deolekr Sahib is my assistant in the office, likewise nobly born. It was in the midst of his broken English (here a squirrel runs down the stairs) that I discovered the £1,000 motor batteries. The works of science are his—all the garages, which I inspected yesterday—imagine me inspecting garages! A monkey nearly bit me and rightly—all wells and cisterns, including the Krishna water works—and the "electric men" (here the squirrel runs back: it has gone to the state drawing room to sit inside a piano). I really must stop now. I will finish this evening and post this at Indore. For I am going in about my clothes to Mhow—over thirty miles' drive each way— "Yes, of course, dear Morgan—any day any car."

Here is the text of the cable he sent my mother on my arrival—

"Your dear son arrived safe last evening, and believe me he is in safe hands and he is in perfect health."

TUKOJIRAO PUAR

I was indeed safe. In no essential did he ever fail me. Quite often I did not understand him—he was too incalculable—but it was possible with him to reach a platform where calculations were unnecessary. It would not be possible with an Englishman.

The day after my arrival we had a bewildering interview and he assigned me my duties: gardens, tennis courts, motors, Guest House, Electric House. None of these had much to do with reading or writing, my supposed specialities. I had an office (hours 7-11 and 4-5). All the post was to pass through my hands. These were not the duties which I had expected or for which I was qualified, but this did not disturb us, and he spent most of the interview in writing me out lists of the dignitaries of state. They fell into four categories: the Ruling Family, the great Maratha nobles, the secondary nobles, and the lesser nobles, who bore the title of Mankari: "in this last lot you will be the first." Reverting to the Ruling Family, he emphasized the names and titles of his brother, his son, his brother's wife, his aunt, and his own absent wife. These were the highest in the land: I was to salaam with two hands and the whole hand, and to extend similar courtesies to the Dewan, the A.G.G. and the P.A. These last two were British officials. I was to regard myself when meeting them as an Indian. But I began by this time to get a little mixed—far from clear for instance as to the composition of the all-powerful Council of State. "Wait a minute!" he cried. On he swept, descending to individual Mankaris and clerks and mysterious persons called "Eighteen Offices" or "Horse Doctor."

"I shall never get all this right," I said.

"Oh yes, you will. Besides it does not matter in the least, except in the case of Brother and those others whom I have specially mentioned."

Then April Fools' Day arrived to reinforce the merriment of Holi. He sent me a message to my office asking me to go at once to a remote shed in the garden since something peculiar had been observed there. I excused myself. Nor, when bidden to refreshment, did I accept a cigarette of unusual shape. Nor was I asked to get an electric shock by sitting on a sofa. But I did drink some whisky-and-salt, to the court's uncategorical delight. Foolery, fun, practical jokes, bawdry—I was to be involved in them all as soon as I felt myself safe. He even made a pun on my name which eludes quotation: too indecent, too silly. But gay, gay.

The suite he assigned me was on the first floor at the end of the drawing-room wing: bedroom, sitting room, anteroom, bathroom, all decently furnished in the European style. It was reached either by a verandah along the inner side of the courtyard, or by a staircase that descended straight into the garden and was sometimes, though not often, locked at the bottom, or by an outside verandah which communicated with the bedroom. It was not very private, but what was? We all of us lived in a passage, the Ruler included. I usually slept on the roof, facing Devi. The nights were increasingly lovely, and I got to know the visiting stars. The constellation of the Lion would often hang exactly above me, the disk of Regulus so large and bright that it resembled a tunnel. So dry was the air that the sheets emitted sparks.

April 6th

Today Malarao Sahib took me to his village. Deolekr Sahib drove the car, and with us came Malarao's cousin, a Sirdar whom I take to a great deal, but who is unfortunately out of favour at court. It is he who lent me Indian clothes on my first visit. He is now a grey-haired young man. The four of us had a pleasant morning and the car did not break down until we were returning. We walked first, along the banks of the Sipra, a deep green river, haunted by sweet skipping birds. There we had an exciting and typical adventure. Our train of villagers stopped and pointed to the opposite bank with cries of a snake. At last I saw it—a black thing reared up to the height of three feet and motionless. I said, "It looks a small dead tree," and was told "Oh no," and exact species and habits of snake were indicated—not a cobra, but very fierce and revengeful, and if we shot it would pursue us several days later all the way to Dewas. We then took stones and threw them across the Sipra (half the width of the Thames at Weybridge) in order to make snake crawl away. Still he didn't move and when a stone hit his base still didn't move. He was a small dead tree. All the villagers shrieked with laughter.

The young Sirdar told them that I was much disappointed and displeased about the snake, and that they must find a real one. So they dispersed anxiously for a few moments over the country, after which all was forgotten.

I call the adventure "typical" because it is even more difficult here than in England to get at the rights of a matter. Everything that happens is said to be one thing and proves to be another, and as it is further said in an unknown tongue I live in a haze. After our walk we returned to the village (150 inhabitants) and I was asked by Malarao and his cousin to select a place to sit down. I avoided a manure heap which had attracted them and we squatted on a mattress beneath a great tree or sat on bedsteads. Cool breeze and all very nice.

We ate enormous cucumbers and drank tea while the villagers sang and tried out of politeness to cover our clothes with red powder. They were an ill-favoured crew, but cheerful. Meanwhile, out of a gap in the village mud-wall, the ladies issued with a strange cry. They, like the red powder, were part of the Hindu festivity of Holi, and squatting at a little distance, they made a bright spot in the dust.

The men continued their songs—one about the coming of Europeans to India, the other about the coming of Man to the Earth. Then my companions made me give the company some rupees (which they afterwards replaced stealthily in my pocket), I chose a site for a house, and we passed into the village by the seated ladies who abused us violently—so violently that even the young Sirdar could not understand what was said. This abuse is of course traditional and has nothing personal in it: 3,000 years ago in Greece the women did just the same thing at certain festivals.

We departed via the temple, where Malarao did a rapid worship for the party generally, then to the car which broke down as aforesaid, and we crawled home, depositing the Sirdar at his house. We had picked him up at it in the morning—of course no one had told him we were coming—and he was stripped for his prayers.

"Come up, Sahib!" he called, leaning from an upper window in this condition. "I was about to pray, but now will not, for it takes a half-hour."

People talk about Oriental seclusion: what strikes me is Oriental publicity. Here I am among Maratha *nobles, a conservative and lofty race, yet I eat with them, sit in their bedrooms and visit their women-folk.*

Arriving as I did during Holi, I found Dewas at its most Dionysiac. That play which I witnessed the first evening at the cavalry tea party was so characteristic of the riotous season that I could not describe it when writing to my suburban home. It was a ribald oriental farce. Husband and wife. She: "Can I go and visit my parents?" He: "Dangerous for you—and for me—and for morality generally." She persists, and as soon as she goes the husband cries, "I want an eunuch. . . ." A tall scraggy man with a moustache then appeared, dressed in a pink sari, and paid grotesque and unwelcome attentions to such members of the audience as H.H. indicated.—This seemed to be a recognised turn.—Squatting beside his victim, the hideous creature sang and mopped and mowed while the court applauded. Returning to the farce, he behaved similarly to the husband and was offering him a present of sweets when the news was brought to the ill-advised wife. She returns from her parents hastily. "How can you ruin your health by such a proceeding?" was her argument, and it prevailed. Since both the performers and the audience were male, H.H. considered that the proprieties had been observed. "If a girl had been acting, it wouldn't have done, it would have been too much. As it is, it was all right." And he commanded a repeat performance that same evening in the Palace.

Holi died down after about a week, the comedians returned to the Deccan, the coloured powders faded, village women ceased to show good will through obscenity, and life became ordinary again, or as ordinary as it could manage to be.

I must now introduce Bai Saheba.

To what extent she was married to the Maharajah I do not know: married she was, but there were extents in Hindu marriages. There were also Golden Concubines and Silver Concubines: when I spoke cautiously and primly about them to him once, he exploded into happy laughter and cried, "She is my Diamond Concubine." She was his refuge after the Kolhapur catastrophe. He seemed devoted to her and I was not surprised. At the time I knew them she had borne him daughters only: later on sons came and helped to complicate life. I shall never know the ins and outs, and I doubt whether any Indian ever grasped them. Intelligent though they are over intrigues, Indians too can get confused and identify hopes with facts. One is reduced—as are they—to siding with the people one likes, and I liked Bai Saheba. She lived in ramshackle quarters at the entrance to the city.

The departed Maharani was seldom mentioned. She lived, I believe, at Kolhapur or in Bombay. We were, however, aware of her family's interest in us. Occasionally a stranger would join our circle: sometimes he was a dignified courtier, sometimes a buffoon, like the Subedhar of my first visit. In either case he was a Kolhapur spy, and I would marvel at the ease with which we received him, and at the lack of reticence we showed in his presence. No doubt we sent our spies to Kolhapur. But these we mentioned never.

April 4th

It has been an awful day. The youngest daughter is ill and I have been sitting with Bai Saheba while the doctors consult. Indeed I must cut this letter short, as I want to send it in to Indore to be posted. I can't go in to meet Masood tomorrow as I hoped, since I

have to keep house or rather palace, in H.H.'s absence.
She does not live here, but in the town, where he is
staying. I like her extremely: most intelligent and
charming. I will write more in detail about her in a
few days. Awful confusion reigns, though Malarao
does his best. Luckily an English doctor—eminent I
think—came to the Guest House for his own con-
venience and has stopped on for ours. I have been
dining with him. Have just sent down cheese and
biscuits to H.H., who appears to eat nothing unless I
provide it. Sometimes I feel I am no use to him, at
others that I am the saving of his life.

The next letter, to Malcolm Darling, is of the nature of a report.

April 12th
I have been here for a fortnight, happy and worried
at once. You will understand either state and laugh at
the worries. So long as I am out for enjoyment, all
contribute to it, but as soon as I try to serve Bapu
Sahib or to make others serve him, I grasp a cloud.
I am glad the arrangement is temporary only; ignorant
of the language and of administration generally, I
could not stop on here permanently. It would not

have been fair. To check the idleness, incompetence and extravagance is quite beyond me. I knew I should find them, but they are far worse than I imagined. It's no use wailing over one's deficiencies— it bores people. I mention them in passing to Bapu Sahib and will do little more than to mention them to you; adding for your private ear that my extra worry is the relationship of so slackly administered a state to the general problem of Indian unrest. If Fate in the form of any political party should ask Dewas a question, what answer could Dewas give?

Bai Saheba I like much and it seems agreeable to all concerned that I should go to see her frequently. She will shortly be confined and poor dear has an old scar further to trouble her. And Prabha Baba has been at death's point—much confusion and wretchedness. Lila and Susila Babas have also been unwell, and I think their house, situate against King Edward VII triumphal arch, is damnable and ought to be condemned. Just at present the batch is convalescent and guzzling chocolates.

Masood is here, having speeded from Hyderabad, and very funny it has been to watch the contest between his heavy premier Moslem artillery and the *light Maratha bowmen, a contest that is conducted with high courtesy on both sides, and I think with mutual respect. He returns to Hyderabad tomorrow. It is very good of him to come in those stewpans of trains.*

Masood (afterwards Sir Syed Ross Masood) was my greatest Indian friend. I had known him since he was an undergraduate at Oxford, and had stayed with him during my first Indian visit. Later on he became vice-chancellor of the University of Aligarh. He came of an eminent Moslem family. His grandfather, Sir Syed Ahmed Khan, had founded Aligarh, his ancestors had been nobles at the Mogul court, and his descent from the Prophet was better documented than that of the Maharajah from the sun.

I had not realised when this important person came to see me at Dewas how dramatic the occasion was. Two extremes were meeting. He had never stayed at a Maratha court before, and the Marathas had never coped with such a guest. There was some nervousness on both sides. On Masood's it took the form of incisiveness and pomposity. He held forth rather too emphatically on the power and wealth of His Exalted

Highness the Nizam of Hyderabad and his salute of twenty-one guns. (We had only fifteen.) Willowy and deferential, Malarao listened to him, making polite sounds. H.H. was also extremely courteous, and behaved almost as to a fellow ruler: there were certain civilites and attentions which Masood had not expected to receive and they gratified him. He was also offered amusements. One day we were sent up Devi on an elephant—which we should have enjoyed more if the howdah had not begun to slip round; human counterweights had to be attached to its fringes or we should have slid backwards, breaking our fall on his nervous Parsi clerk and on my own clerk, who were our pendents behind. "I prefer not to be on a tower when the base totters," said Masood majestically. The elephant kept covering his head with spray, as in Buddhist sculpture. The Parsi clerk, whom we expected to faint, became all animation during the ordeal, and told many droll tales about the customs of elephants, "who if treated ill may become, sir, extremely unruly."

Another day we were despatched in a car to Ujjain, in Gwalior territory, where the operations of a holy riverside were in full swing—hundreds of saddhus in cream grey or ochrous ash, carefully dressed in their own fashion, and interested in passing events even when sitting on spikes. One (in dove) was laughing at a joke, another (sooty with tawny hair) was annoyed at something, and two or three were entertaining each other to tea. "My dear chap, I ask you!" said Masood, as if it was my fault. Those saddhus would sometimes come to Dewas and bless the Palace, and demand a hundred rupees each. Malarao would speak them as fair as he could and give each of them one rupee. They then cursed the Palace and returned to Ujjain.

After three days of Hinduism, Masood retired with his clerks and his files to Hyderabad. Our incompetence distressed him more than it could me because he saw it as an extreme example of his country's inefficiency.

My chronicle to my mother resumes:

April 17th
Last night I went for a solitary and very lovely drive at sunset to a big garden belonging to the state, and watched the storks flying over the mango trees, and poked at the termite ant hills that jut up like little

dolomites out of the soil. On getting back I found
Bai Saheba with H.H. She was in good health and
spirits. These high-class Indian ladies deserve all that
has been written about them. At present I am a little
uncritical, all seeming so delicate in their form and
so expressive in their gestures, whether of face or
garment. But Bai Saheba seems so good and sweet:
and she is dramatic in her way of talk and must be
amusing if you know the language, which (it is
Marathi) I never shall know. Your picture, looking
rather sneering, was exhibited, and I was asked why,
at my advanced age, I had not married. Later on,
I brought her a chair for her feet, as she looked as
if she'd like one. Much pleased she exclaimed: "May
you find a wife waiting for you when you return, and
may you have a son"—a common blessing. H.H. was
sick, so I escorted her to her carriage. Straw screens
were let down over the windows, and she again became the remote Oriental lady, with soldiers gal-
loping behind.

H.H. fancying he would sleep better in the state
drawing room, we now repaired to that apartment.
When we turned on the electric light a servant,
stripped to the waist, was discovered slumbering. He

was ejected and a vast mattress spread on the floor, over it a delicate sheet, a big pillow and a side pillow for each arm. But before he could lie down, more horses were heard in the courtyard, and his sister-in-law, with a train of handmaids, was reported approaching.

"Tiresome woman and so restless—no, I must see her. I will introduce her—stop as long as you are not bored—then the general will dandle her."

She also was graceful and small, in a pink sari. After a few civilities he lay down on his drawing-room-floor bed, and she perched on the edge, full of solicitude.

"Play patience, all of you, if you will," he commanded, "it may relieve me."

Cards were brought and we played patience all over the carpet. The lady and I did one together, the general, the veterinary surgeon and the district officer played in the distance. Ours was soon over, owing to the puerile latitude of the rules, which have been modified, I suppose, to suit harem mentality. Failure was impossible. Then I rose and left the strange scene. Holy songs arose from the drawing room later. Sister-in-law had retired at last, and some of the court were chanting Marathi hymns to their sovereign while others massaged his calves. Amid their ministrations he fell into a doze.

The third great lady of the state, the Dowager Maharani, I have not yet met. She had not heard of his illness, or she would have been all over us too. The three hate one another—triangular—you can call it a quadrilateral if you count the vanished Maharani, now biding with her father at Kolhapur. Sister-in-law came again this afternoon, now with her husband, and while the brothers talked she and I essayed English. Conversation on artistic and literary lines. Sister-in-law paints "partly in London partly in Indian style." Also plays chess and has promised to teach me the Indian variety tomorrow evening. Since Bai Saheba has been invited to dine, they will clash, and perhaps have a row.

I cannot get over the constant publicity. Even when the doors are made to shut they do not, owing to warping; and, servants not thinking it polite to knock, you may any time find yourself amid creeping forms. Plenty of sentries, but they generally sleep face downward. We lie as open to the countryside as to

one another. It is indescribable and unimaginable—
really a wonderful experience, for it is the fag end
of a vanished civilisation. But my brain seems as
messy as its surroundings, and I cannot realise it at
all. Also the crude ugliness of this palace presses on
me. It's a relief to get out in the evening, for once
away I am among wonderful trees and birds.

The temperature has touched 104°, which is only
four below our summer maximum. So I feel relieved,
because I do not find the heat excessive. I have got
tatties for my room and have found a little boy with
a huge turban who throws water on them from the
outside verandah—sometimes so violently that he
drenches me as I sit within. The tatties, though made
to measure, bear no relation to their apertures. But
I have propped them on a pile of bricks, which bricks
were brought up out of chaos on the heads of another
little boy and three little girls. I am very solemn
about making myself comfortable, and Malarao is
most kind. The dryness is great—I forget if I told you
that my best clothes crackled in the evening, and gave
me an electric shock, and that my locked diary and
other books were warped, but they got better. A wine-
glassful of liquid evaporates in three days, and the

fate of ink is desperate. It's this, rather than heat, that strikes me.

Another report to Malcolm:

April 24th

Since my last letter I have been reading aloud (M. Arnold's Essays mostly), which has made me feel more useful. What intelligence, what subtlety, and what a memory! Bapu Sahib's, I mean. He follows all allusions to Greek mythology, and he cannot have heard them since your tutorial epoch. So am happier and will proceed to the latest intrigue. Not that I am very happy about that, because one of the best people in the state (to my mind) is its centre—that young Sirdar Waghalkar. He has much character and ability, and I like him, but Bapu Sahib holds him in displeasure. I want him sent away—he is too independent and restless to fit into the Dewas I see. But Bapu Sahib proposes to keep him under his eye and says he can't send him away and allow him to retain his jagir. Malarao, who is Household Member on the Council, is Sirdar Sahib's cousin and under his influence—that's one irritant. And there are others into which it is not here convenient to go. But if you looked in here in July, you could in this as in all things be quite useful! It is a problem of character, and tricksiness cannot solve it, and this you could make Bapu Sahib see.

The enclosed * is more amusing because (as I remarked in my inaugural speech), "If it fails, the foundations of the state will not be shattered." Our meeting was not unduly successful. Mr. Shastri brought some of his guile as well as all his heart, and raised the vernacular question with the intent of becoming himself Assistant Secretary or, failing that, interpreter. Myself (Secretary) was cold to such kind offers and predicted the death of the Society if once it contracted Bilingualitis. Then came the social problem. Should lofty lineage and official eminence or should knowledge of English be the test! The Dewan came out as a democrat, or to be more precise as an antipalatine. So the schoolmasters have been let in but the merchants hang in the balance, which is the best one can expect in the best of all possible courts.

Weather remains very decent. Tatties work well, though the cisterns are so low that a little fish was

* My manifesto on the subject of a Dewas Literary Society.

thrown against them out of a bucket. The bhisti's child extracted it and brought it to me, for which I praised him and now it lives permanently on the verandah. Exactly what part the lower animals play in my system I know not yet, but it gave me a shock to meet a tortoise in the Krishna water works. It sat on the central slab—Vishnu himself no doubt. Now I drink soda water. Of course the tortoises of Indore have sat in that, but I do not see them, any more than I see the cooking of our Indian khana. It doesn't do to think. To follow the promptings of the eye and the imagination is quite complicated enough.

Political Agent Adams, wife and daughter, come this evening, and are located by my machinations in the Guest House, not in the Palace, whither was their high intention. They will be more comfortable in the Guest House, but that was not my main object. I want—as Bapu Sahib wants—the Palace to be reserved for his personal friends, and I would thwart this official jollity which exclaims, "You took in Luard, Maharajah Sahib, now you must take in me." Moreover, a cow has to be milked in person before the person of Political Agent Adams, otherwise he will feel uneasy about his tea, and it is far more delicate that

*this should take place out of my sight. However we
don't worry much about the Adamses. Our horror
and our joy is the possibility of a visit from Scindhia,
who having drunk the waters at Ujjain where 3,000,-
000 saddhus had been bathing, may proceed here
with both his wives, and develop cholera at his leisure.*

The Dewas Literary Society arose out of Macaulay's
essay on Frederick the Great. I had been reading to
H.H., Macaulay's account of the adventures of Vol-
taire at the tyrant's court, and we were both struck by
the piquant parallel. Here was I a literary man at his
court, and presumably in his power. A resident Vol-
taire, ought I not to do something?

So I drew up a manifesto, which still survives. Its
tone is intentionally formal. I informed my Maratha
peers that there are two reasons for the pursuit of
literature: it introduces the reader to the noble writ-
ings of the past and the present, and it introduces him
to other readers, similarly employed. Our proceedings
were to be in English, but works in other languages
would also be discussed. No subscription would be
necessary, only sympathy and practical support. The
first meeting would be held on April 20th at 7:30 in

the front room, ground floor, north wing, Shri Anand Bhuvan Palace. "Will the undermentioned gentlemen (most of whom I have the pleasure and privilege of knowing personally) be so kind as to signify whether they will support the scheme, and attend the meetings when their other engagements permit?" The names of about two dozen nobles followed. All signified their support, most of them proved to have other engagements. Still a few meetings were held before we petered out.

I remember a paper of my own where I quoted that story out of Dostoevsky about the wicked woman and the onion. She had been so wicked that in all her life she had only done one good deed—given an onion to a beggar. So she went to hell. As she lay in torment she saw the onion, lowered down from Heaven by an angel. She caught hold of it. He began to pull her up. The other damned saw what was happening and caught hold of it too. She was indignant and cried, "Let go—it's my onion," and as soon as she said "my onion" the stalk broke and she fell back into the flames.

I had always thought this story touching, but I had no idea of the effect it would produce on the Dewas

Literary Society. Hitherto they had been polite, bored, straining to follow. Now their faces softened, and they murmured, "Ah that is good, good. That is *bhakti*." They had encountered something that they loved and understood. I have often thought of that moment since—that flash of comprehension in the midst of India. Of the many English writers I had quoted, not one had touched them. Their hearts were unlocked by a Russian.

April 28th

Three days' visit from Colonel Adams, his wife and his daughter, are mercifully over—not that anyone could have been more pleasant than the two ladies. Adams was whiskified and fishy-faced, and obviously a bully, though the changed status of the native states did not give him much scope, and I sometimes patted back. They stopped at the Guest House, where a special cow had to attend them and be milked in their presence, but they came up here for lunch and dinner. Various Government servants came with them and demanded from us money for food (which we gave, though there is an official circular forbidding the request) and money for the journey from Indore to

Dewas and back, which I had much pleasure in refusing—it would have been given if I had not been here
and they would also have exacted tips. Hints to
Adams produce no effect. His predecessor put down
all such abuses, but he thinks it fitting that the native
should be spoiled and teased and expected me to be
amused by his witty tales of his servants' sharp prac-
tices. I hear that his superior—also a "Colonel" at
Indore—is even his inferior in deportment.

It is strange that the Political Department, which
has to deal with princes, should specialise in bad manners. It was just the same ten years ago, though it is
less painful now, as the princes are more uppish. I
don't see, nor am I likely to see, anything of present
movements in India, except indirectly: I mean that
the Government, frightened of Bolshevism and Gandhi, is polite to the princes, and the princes, equally
frightened, do all that they can to stop the spread of
new ideas. There are said to be new ideas, even in
Dewas, but they are not perceptible to a Western
eye. Politically—though not socially—we are still living in the fourteenth century. Masood was scared at
our backwardness and had a conversation (very polite)

with H.H. on the point. A new constitution is to be drafted, so that the people may be educated gradually, but a new constitution was being drafted when I was here ten years ago, and if the people ever get educated it will be from outside. They look happy, work in moderation, and block the roads with bullock carts, which deploy in fan formation as soon as they hear a motor approaching. This palace, with its warped pianos and broken telephones, is really only an excrescence on the ancient countryside, and I love driving away from it in the evening to a garden about two miles off, where everything is peaceful and I can sit on the edge of a cistern under huge trees.

While the Adamses were here, the motor expert, with wife and little girl, arrived from Indore, and I had to fly to and fro like a shuttlecock. They were nice people—Manchester—and H.H. asked them to our banquet of "haute politique" from which I had assumed they would be excluded. All went well, and Mrs. and Miss Adams were excessively nice. Adams, when he saw them first in the distance at the Guest House, exclaimed: "Who the devil are those people?" (Pretty manners when he was himself a guest.) But we made Adams behave. The expert gave some sound advice, none of which will be adopted. The thing to do is to have an expert, and there the matter ends.

I could never describe the muddle in this place. It is wheel within wheel. Pipes have been laid (for example) all down the flower border, and connected with an empty water tank, which stands on four legs and takes its share in spoiling our surroundings. It is connected—in its turn—with an almost empty well, and if there was any water in the well it would be raised into the tank by an electric pump of insufficient power to raise the water. You are not at the end of the chain yet, for the electric pump is connected with the Electric House which is only on at night, when all its energies are required for the Palace lighting. So there we are, and there are the flowers dying. I tried to raise the water from the well by bullocks, but only one pair could be found, and one of them was so ill that I sent it to Indore to the Hospital for Indisposed Cows. (We are not supposed to kill even a fly.) I said, "I sent," which sounds very grand, but it meant three days' worrying before the poor creature was driven off. Blasting operations are the last stage. The electric pump has been removed, and a shower of men, women and children have been

dropped into the well where they pash up what remains of the water and make horrible smells with gun-
powder.

April 30th

Baldeo is here! Blacker and more wizened than I remember him, but certainly Baldeo. We met with
transports of moderate affection and at present all is
energy and devotion. But I expect that, having too
little to do, he will become tiresome. He seems not
to have eaten since his arrival twenty-four hours ago,
and not greatly to mind. Religion the obstacle. The
court is not strict, and Baldeo wants a room for himself where he can cook his food. He will have to go
over to a hut by the well, which is tiresome. H.H. is
very pleasant to him.

✺ BIRTH OF A BABY ✺

May 9th

The birth of a little baby has turned everything upside down, so far as it wasn't already in that position.
The rites—they are more than customs—are extraordinary, and seem designed to cause the greatest possible discomfort to mother and child. The unfortu-

nate pair have to listen to music outside their door for nearly fifteen days. It began with fireworks and a discharge of rifles from the entire army in batches: then drums, trumpets, stringed instruments and singing. For five days the husband is supposed not to see his wife, but during the whole fifteen he must sleep in the compound where her house stands and his friends and attendants stay with him and listen to the continual music. So here I am. I come down from the Palace after dinner and squat amid discordant sounds till I fall asleep. My bed is next to H.H.'s, Malarao's on the other side. The courtyard is tidier than it was, but the first night we lay with bullocks all around.

Yesterday being the fifth day the music did go on all night. Nautch girls and boys dressed as girls howled, there were farces, dialogues, dances, the military band moaned Western melodies. I went to bed at midnight, but at 3 A.M. something unusual aroused me—the music became beautiful; so I fitted on my turban and rejoined the company. H.H. was asleep on his bed, the townsfolk had gone off to their homes, and only a few experts survived. Why save your best singers until 3 A.M.? "Ask India another" is the only answer to such a question! I am as far as ever from understanding Indian singing, but have no doubt that I was listening to great art, it was so complicated and yet so passionate. The singer (man) and the drummer were of almost equal importance and wove round the chord of C major elaborate patterns that came to an end at the same moment—at least that's as near as I can explain it: it was like Western music reflected in trembling water, and it continued in a single burst for half an hour. The words were unimportant, mere excuses for the voice to function.

But what fun the lady and the little baby get out of the above I don't know. H.H. quite agrees that it is monstrous—he has all the right feelings—but says tradition is too strong to be changed! At one time the band was actually in the bedroom. The courtiers haven't even the feelings. One of them, when I suggested that a fortnight's row is not the best of starts, replied, "Why so? It will prevent the mother from sadness. It is not as if she was ill"!! If it had been a boy baby the noises would have been doubled and the bill for festivities have reached £2,000, instead of the modest £1,000 that is anticipated at present. We need the money elsewhere and the work of the state is being postponed.

I am to see Bai Saheba this evening. She has been much pleased that I sleep down here, for she appreciates the din and the mass of males. I have just had my salary for April, not through the finance department but from the Superintendent of Police, who playfully poured 300 silver rupees into my topi.

May 17th

We culminated on May 15th with terrific and grotesque festivities, leaving our previous efforts nowhere. The chief feature was the presentation of gifts to the mother and child. H.H. was so very nice—told me about it, so that I might not be left out, and secretly assisted me in my choice. I rested in the morning, and drove down to Bai Saheba's to change into Indian clothes, then drove on with my gifts to join forces with the Commander in Chief and his gifts. Malarao, the Chief of Police, etc., etc., swelled the party, and we marched back to Bai Saheba's on foot, first the army, playing the "British Grenadiers," then servants, bearing the gifts on platters, then ourselves, hand in hand in affable converse, then a huge crowd, and finally the Commander in Chief's lady in a purdah carriage. As we reached Bai Saheba's, two other bands struck up, one military but making Indian sounds, the other the violent bangbang of the Sweepers, outcastes but loyal subjects who stood at the side of the road hitting sieves with shovels. We swept into the courtyard, then melted into nothing, as is the Indian spirit. There was no grand crisis or reception.

The gifts were dumped on a durry, where, very anxious, sat H.H., among clerical assistants. For he had to give back to each donor a gift of equal value, and quickly to guess what each present cost. I gave the lady a sari for day wear and a piece of silk for a jacket, and to the baby a deplorable piece of pink material. This was a respectable minimum gift: near relatives added coconuts, silver ornaments, and rice. While we all messed on the durry, the ladies kept arriving, mostly in covered ox wagons, and were decanted into the purdah tent beside us. The gifts couldn't be taken in because of the Dowager Maharani, who as always was late. A cradle arrived, made by the state carpenters, and very dizzy in its action. H.H. had meant to get me almost into the purdah tent, but desisted, as a few old-fashioned people would have minded. We went into the house behind, against which the tent backed, and I sat by the door and peeped over his shoulder, but saw little. He worked like an under-waiter in a Soho restaurant. The platters came out through the door of the purdah tent, containing the gifts that had been submitted and approved, and he upset them—clothes, coconuts and all —upon the floor where we sat, in order to leave the platter free for the return service. His return gift was popped on, and back it went into purdah to the wife of the man who made the original gift. Having no wife—or none on the spot—I got my return present direct. I had chosen it beforehand—a goldified turban which he told me was the proper monetary equivalent of what I had given. I was pleased: not so the Dowager Maharani, who rejected her return present because she thought it only cost 200 rupees, whereas there was precedent for 250 rupees. This, and other bad news, kept leaking out through the folds of the tent. H.H. was sad but philosophic: "I spend all this money in the hope they would be happy, but they quarrel— it always happens . . . yes, the Dowager Maharani has been rude, but how can I take any notice? They will think it revenge for her behaviour in the past to me and she is defenceless now. I shall invite her later on for the singing . . ."—all the time pouring valuables onto the dusty floor. I grew hungry and rummaged for candy and monkey nuts.

Inside, the child was "named" Pudmawatai Baba. She will be Pudma for short. Her name should contain the astrological letter indicated by her horoscope, but the horoscope indicated Z which was found difficult and abandoned. We could hear her crying in the new cradle, and her sisters also wept on account of the heat and had to be extracted. They came out lolling over the backs of servants, and looking like gorgeously dressed but unstuffed dolls. Bai Saheba— of whom I failed to catch a glimpse—was also suffering from the heat and from the quarrels of her ladies: she sweltered in a sari that was almost total gold.

Now I come to the banquet. The ladies had theirs first, and it was 11 P.M. before we sat down in the courtyard (really a farmyard) to cold rice, etc., all rather nasty. It didn't last long, to my relief, for squatting becomes more difficult as the years go by. The singing followed, but could not start because the Dowager Maharani would not come: getting on for 1 A.M. before she issued from the purdah tent in a moveable box of curtains, and was put into a hut with a semitransparent curtain, close to our proceedings. She summoned the chief singer—a Gwalior lady and excessively good—and began to talk to her through the curtain and presently to weep with her, for the Maharajah of Gwalior's mother, now deceased and a friend to both, came into the conversation and touched a tender chord.

At this point I remarked to H.H., "If I were king, I'd stand no more of this."

"Give any order you like, Morgan," he replied plaintively.

So we sent for another singer, but before he came the reminiscences of Gwalior ended and the entertainment began. I was too much exhausted to listen long, and retired to a bed. An immense ox lay close beside me, so close that when my foot—the bed was too small—shot out at the end, I touched its hump. It was very friendly and polite and did not make trouble until a dog got under the bed and barked at it, when it swayed its head. Somewhere about three the Dowager Maharani went, and the beds were dragged into a smarter part of the yard.

The Dowager Maharani—Tara Raja was her name—
had long been known to me as Dewas-Nuisance-Lady
No. 1. Widow to the previous ruler, she had supported her nephew's elevation to the throne, but once
he was there did nothing but vex him. Malcolm's
early letters are full of her. A row about a silver spoon,
which she accused her English companion of stealing,
shook the court from top to bottom, and there was
still greater trouble over the state jewels which she
annexed, and was obliged to give up on his marriage.
She squabbled with his mother, she danced dressed
as a man with her maidservants similarly dressed, she
was unruly and bizarre, and she tried to poison him.
So he alleged, and that was why he had been so re-
luctant to visit her at Malcolm's behest.

I never could accept the poison story—there seemed
no conceivable motive for the crime—but H.H. believed it himself in a far-off way, and declared that
at one time he had always made her eat before he
did, when they ate together, though now this was not
necessary, also that a dog had once expired. By now
he felt no fear, no resentment, no hostility. All that
persisted was a faint malaise, a sort of accentuated
boredom, a disinclination to entertain her personally.

"Oh blast, her Dowager Highness again," he would cry, as her carriage rolled into the compound. "No, I cannot, I simply cannot. You must, Morgan," and I had several tête-à-têtes with her in consequence.

She was gracious and amiable to me, also homely, and she had that slight air of despair that suits an Indian lady so well, showing no resentment, only the disillusionment with which a well-bred person faces all life. In appearance she was short and dumpy, but there was nothing grotesque about her: her sari was on the sober side, her expression frank and resigned, and if she did not talk English perfectly she anyhow expressed herself perfectly in English. As we poured out tea, or she the tea and I the milk, as we offered one another bread and butter, or blew the flies off the little cakes, I can never have come nearer to banqueting with Catherine de' Medici.

Like other Indian ladies of that period her Dowager Highness was an expert at semi-purdah. She had practised it at her great-niece's birth festival, and I remember another occasion in the large drawing room when we were listening to a military band. The noise woke her up in a distant part of the palace and she wanted to come. A shelter was rigged up behind a screen, and she was conveyed to it, wrapped in a sheet. After a little she became restless, peeped round the edge of the screen and saw another which might suit her better. So she made a dart, taking cover en route behind a chair. Arrived at the second screen she sat down on the carpet again and felt hungry. Refreshments were ordered and she flitted a second time. Again she crouched behind the chair, to arise in a more modern mood, and to stroll towards the food in full view of the band.

She came from Kolhapur but had also her Gwalior connection—Malcolm was dubious as to its exact character. At the time I knew her, her age was about fifty. She died in 1930, in the Old Palace.

✑ SCINDHIA'S VISIT ⤢

The visit of Scindhia, Maharajah of Gwalior, followed soon after the baby's birth, and my letters refer to his expected arrival, his non-arrival, and his actual arrival at Dewas. He was a vigorous and vulgar prince, and being both H.H.'s neighbour and his uncle, had acquired considerable influence over him. Malcolm believed the influence to be bad, and had had an unpleasant experience during their All-India tour:

Scindhia, with a mixture of blarney and bluff, had got hold of his young pupil and practically held him a prisoner in the Gwalior palace. There was a terrific row. Since the break with Kolhapur the influence had, if anything, increased. Scindhia could not boast of lofty lineage, for his ancestor had been but the Peshwa's slipper-bearer, but he was everything that seemed up to date at Dewas: a shrewd man of business, a forceful politician, he could drive a railway train in dashing fashion, and if the passengers expressed alarm he could proclaim, "No danger, Scindhia drives." His little boy and girl (called at that time George and Mary) had already honoured us, the boy as a Tommy in khaki, and now he himself was expected at Ujjain, with both his Maharanis, to bathe in the Sipra.

A cordial invitation had been despatched without results. H.H. then decided that we must go to Ujjain ourselves, pay our compliments, and persuade him to come. It should not be difficult—he was so genial and jolly. We set forth in all our available cars, picking up the Dowager Maharani en route. She was an essential item in the embassy because of her Gwalior connection. She lived a little way out of the city, in a sort of zareba near the Krishna water works. Twisting this way and that between purdah screens, we extricated her, and proceeded.

At Ujjain we passed a most ignoble evening. The great man wouldn't say yes and wouldn't say no, he teased and he swanked, sometimes H.H. implored him, sometimes the Dowager Maharani, sometimes he was the object of a general prayer. At one point in the discussion a slipshod dinner was served, and I remember that when it came to smoking and I wanted a match, Scindhia bounced the match box at me on the tablecloth although he was near enough to hand it. That gesture, and his brusque questionings as to my status, were in striking contrast to the unbroken courtesy and gentleness of Dewas. How I thanked my stars!

An enormous wait followed the meal, during which I lost everyone. Presently I saw the Dowager Maharani alone in a side room. Scindhia had plied her with brandy, and she was drunk. "Not good of His Highness, not right of him, it is his joke," she sighed, and complained that her feet hurt. I suggested that she should put them up on a chair and lifted them onto one. "What a funny thing to do!" and she smiled at me doubtfully. We remained together in that odd harmony which India occasionally provides. When she tried to arise I dissuaded her and soothed her. "It's all right, Your Highness, it doesn't matter, it can't be helped," and she echoed, "Can't be helped, but not good of him."

After midnight our own Maharajah joined us. He looked pale and worried. Victory—Scindhia had agreed to come. But where were all the cars? They had all gone back to Dewas, each supposing us to be in another one. Only a small Ford remained. The three of us squeezed into the back seat, the Dowager in the middle. She passed out. He looked at me across her collapsed back and said, "Now, my dear Morgan, now, you begin to realise some of my problems."

May 24th
We have had much expensive and uninspiriting nonsense to do honour to the Maharajah of Gwalior, who has paid us a twelve hours' visit, which I did not find too short. Since he likes singing, H.H. would order singers from Bombay though warned it was risky. Sure enough, the singers caught too late a train, and are arriving now, when the whole Gwalior party has

left. *They are at the top of their tree (i.e., it is like ordering Ternini, etc. to come to Weybridge from Berlin), and they will wear jewels worth thousands of pounds, with none but my drooping eyes to regard them. Partly through fatigue, partly through thoughts of the misery in England and elsewhere, I feel glum and disapproving. One can go too far down the "primrose path" and we have done so on this occasion. Moreover, Maharajah Gwalior was a bounder, so there has been no satisfaction in any direction, at least from my point of view. It is poor work at the best of times, spending money on rich men.*

I make further complaint in a letter to Lowes Dickinson.

May 31st
Scindhia is in private life an insolent and surly buffoon and in public a militarist and an obscurantist. The Maharajah idealises him and adores him like a school-girl, and the influence explains all or nearly all I don't like in his character. It was very illuminating. Much that had puzzled me by its inharmoniousness has become clear—the tiresome practical jokes, the growing dread of education, the bawdy talk which is subtly

wrong—I can see their origin, and they are to some extent faults of taste. In fact I was coming round a little to your view of the Indian or anyhow the Hindu character—that it is unaesthetic. One is starved by the absence of beauty. The one beautiful object I can see is something no Indian has made or can touch—the constellation of the Scorpion which now hangs at night down the sky. I look forward to it as to a theatre or picture gallery after the constant imperfections of the day.

Anyhow the visit was not a success. "Above all we must not convey the impression of disorganisation. It can be done." But it had not been done, the electric lights had fused, an electric man's ears had been boxed, the singers from Indore, called in when the Bombay girls failed to arrive, had been deplorable. And there was none of the jolly romping I had been promised: uncle and nephew were supposed to be such pals. They exchanged some perfunctory buffets, but never got going. What he wanted from a person so inferior to himself, I do not know. He had a craving to be liked, and perhaps the very inferiority of the other person stimulated it.

✧§ THE RAINS §✧

May 31st

Electricity filled today. The head engineer of the company, a pretentious and plausible person, who retains his military title, has been up from Bombay with his wife, and I have floundered about mains and switches and standards and carburetors and I don't know what. I took up the safest line I could see—said I knew nothing at all but implied I had much general intelligence. I hoped thus to make him a little nervous. The batteries are still not installed in the power house, because eleven of their glass boxes have been smashed in transit.

Simla is the next event. H.H. is going to see and possibly to stay with Lord Reading, and means to take me with him. I hope to get off—Chhatarpur presses me to come and it would be a good opportunity. I can't face important people any more, I find. Indeed I would much rather stay in Dewas altogether until the heat breaks. Here it is bearable, almost pleasant, because of the cool winds. Elsewhere everyone is in torment and it is no use climbing up for a couple of days to Simla if one is tortured all the way there and *back in the trains. In a fortnight the monsoon ought to break—then all will be cooler—and damper too, and the roads will be dotted with tortoises and frogs. I have got some flower seeds which I shall scatter over the dusty plain that we call the garden. People say they will come up. Both the wells are dry, and the municipal water is cut off most of the day. Baldeo makes a frightful fuss because the bath won't fill, and he dislikes extra trouble. I am lordly and repeat, "I must have my bath," until he gets the tennis boys and they steal the empty fire buckets and dip them in the ornamental fountain among the fish and carry them dripping up the staircase. And so it goes on.*

The above letter mentions the visit of the engineer of the Electric Company and his lady. So prosaic in itself, it involved a mysterious incident. I have often puzzled over the incident, and it is not the only time that I have wondered whether the Maharajah might possess supernormal faculties. The couple were on their second visit to us, and incidentally mentioned an adventure that had happened to them after their first visit. They were motoring away from Dewas to Indore, and just as they crossed the Sipra some animal or other dashed out of the ravine and charged their car so that it swerved and nearly hit the parapet of the bridge.

His Highness sat up, keenly interested. "The animal came from the left?" he asked.

"Yes."

"It was a large animal? Larger than a pig but not as big as a buffalo?"

"Yes, but how did you know?"

"You couldn't be sure what animal it was?"

"No, we couldn't."

He leant back again and said, "It is most unfortunate. Years ago I ran over a man there. I was not at all to blame—he was drunk and ran onto the road and I was cleared at the enquiry, and I gave money to his family. But ever since then he has been trying to kill me in the form you describe."

The three of us were awestruck. But he had told the story in an ordinary tone of voice and went on to ordinary things. On another occasion he told me of some witches that he had surprised at their work, on another of the tiny points of light that appear all over the Himalayas when the holy men light their fires.

On another occasion, when he was staying down at
Bai Saheba's, he appeared to know what was occurring
up in the New Palace before he had been informed.
He was both shrewd and imaginative, and the combination explains much. But in the case of the Sipra
animal there is an unexplained residuum.

June 1st

*Harassed night. Dog barked furiously—supposed
thieves. H.H. very alert and gay as always on such
occasions, and told me long yarns about his uncle, the
late ruler; a comet had fallen at his death, as happens
when great men pass away. This was at one. I went
up to bed again and was nearly blown out of it by a
hurricane at three and at five the birds awoke and
disputed about nesting arrangements, and the squir-
rels fought. What draws animals to this wilderness of
dust and mortar I can't imagine. There are—in the
distance—some quite nice trees.—I will stop now, for
the chaprassi (messenger) is going and must take this
to the post. He is in rags and what survives of his
clothes yellow with stains. I had something to say but
I can't remember what. The washerman tears my own
clothes to pieces—it is lucky I wear so few.*

June 4th

Today—King-Emperor's Birthday—there was a formal Durbar. I wore a long dressing gown of palish purple spattered with gold flowers and beneath it a green waistcoat, also begolded, and on my head a fantastic headdress of red and gold; also white trousers; and the dressing gown and waistcoat were trimmed with red that was supposed to match the turban but did not. I thought I looked a perfect ass (was much admired) but you will see for yourself, for these clothes really are my own, being flung together desperately for the occasion. I have quite an Indian wardrobe now. It was a chair-durbar—no squatting. The telegram to the King-Emperor was read by the Dewan, "God Save the King" was excruciatingly rendered, attar and pan were handed round, and there followed a pleasant tea party.

The day before I spent in a more Western way, paying bills. I got hold of 1,500 rupees (i.e., £100; I don't know where it came from—I am rather good at getting hold of money) and banged it all away, settling small accounts—I cannot tackle the large ones. I cannot grasp the finances of the state. I am told they are admirable. They may be, but they do not look

136

it. The treasury, so far as I have observed, pays nobody and nothing. But a loud lamentation, in which
I am now expert, often raises a bag of silver coins, or
even two or three bags, which Baldeo carries to my
bedroom and inters in various boxes. Sometimes there
is not even a bag, but the coins lie in a heap in the
courtyard, a crowd around them. Then Baldeo brings
linen boot-bags, and we load them up.

Simla sounds imminent. I trust there will be some
hitch, for I dread stirring out of this bearable, and
sometimes delightful, climate, and frying in a train.
Masood writes, as always affectionately, wanting me
to come and stop. It will be curious to see something
of the India that is changing. There is no perceptible
change here, indeed the atmosphere is in some ways
less Western than it was nine years ago. No one,
except myself, wears European clothes, for instance
—nine years ago H.H. often did. The place is altogether exceptional, and generalisations from it, which
I am sure to make, are sure to be wrong. There is no
anti-English feeling. It is Gandhi whom they dread
and hate.

I have just written a long letter to Colonel Wilson,
who has complained with some heat that no one writes

to him as they promised. Though I never promised I have stepped in and told him much that he must know or will not want to know. In the latter category comes my news that he cannot have a garden without water, and that in consequence he cannot have a garden. Our Public Works Officer, a plump and sanguine man, rather nice, bustled up last week crying that all our troubles were over, for we could tap "The Well that Speaks," and off we drove to look at it. But it said nothing to the purpose, since it was choked with mud, and would require elaborate arrangement of pumps and pipes, the latter carried under two roads, and estimates for the work rose rapidly from tens of rupees to hundreds and thence to thousands. So "The Well that Speaks" has relapsed into silence again.

Mangoes! Have never mentioned them. Large ones from Bombay and little ones locally. The large ones you cut in three—it is only the central section that requires the proverbial bath. The little ones you imbibe like an orange. There are not many other strange fruits, but the Jack fruits are ripening a little—they are extraordinary, with crocodile scales. I am told *that they taste delicious but smell awful, so that it is torture until they are actually in your mouth.*

There was a hitch over Simla, and we remained comfortably at home for the coming of the rains. I have pieced together two or three letters describing that event; dates, June 12th—20th.

The first shower was smelly and undramatic. Now there is a new India—damp and grey, and but for the unusual animals I might think myself in England. The full monsoon broke violently, and upon my undefended form. I was under a little shelter in the garden, sowing seeds in boxes with the assistance of two aged men and a little boy. I saw black clouds and felt some spots of rain. This went on for a quarter of an hour, so that I got accustomed to it, and then a wheel of water swept horizontally over the ground. The aged men clung to each other for support. I don't know what happened to the boy. I bowed this way and that as the torrent veered, wet through of course, but anxious not to be blown away like the roof of palm leaves over our head. When the storm decreased or rather became perpendicular, I set out for the Palace, large boats of mud forming on either foot. A rescue expedition, consisting of an umbrella and a servant, set out to meet me, but the umbrella blew inside out and the servant fell down.

Since then there have been some more fine storms, with lightning very ornamental and close. The birds fly about with large pieces of paper in their mouths. They are late, like everyone else, in their preparations against the rough weather, and hope to make a nest straight off, but the wind blows the paper round their heads like a shawl, and they grow alarmed and drop it. The temperature is now variable, becomes very hot between the storms, but on the whole things have improved. I feel much more alert and able to concentrate. The heat made me so stupid and sleepy, though I kept perfectly well.

We have had cholera in the city—a very little, still it was a worry, and I went into Indore and was re-inoculated to be perfectly safe. My colleagues rather despised me for doing this—thought me cowardly and impious, for if one is to die of cholera one will die. Now the worry is over, as the rain has flushed out the drains. There were no cases in the Palace, which stands in a healthy waste, uncontaminated by even a tree.

Now's the time for seed sowing, but like the birds I am not ready. I could not get the manure or, rather, could not get carts in which to fetch it. The roads were blocked with carts, bullocks, buffaloes, by the thousand. But no cart, bullock or buffalo could be got for His Highness. At last I got bullocks—unattached to carts, so they merely ate. Then a cart came, one of whose wheels was six inches larger than the other. I lost my temper, which is all to the good in this place. At last we are suited, but Nature has not waited for our difficulties, and the beds are not manured. Some of the boxes have been, and I am sowing my sixty packets of seed in them. I am mildly interested in the seeds, not keenly, having now too much knowledge of the future. Someone will lie down on the boxes for a sleep.

Simla is off, I think: anyhow now that the weather has broken the expedition will be tolerable. H.H. wants Lord Reading to open the new constitution, and if he accepts there will be a constitution, if he refuses it will probably shrink to the annual birthday speech, in which vast changes are annually announced.

Part of my gardening consists in catching cows and

*despatching them to the pound. The aged gardener,
four little tennis boys and self yesterday cornered a
very lively animal, all horns, feet and tail. We
wreathed its face in rope which broke, it kicked out,
tennis boys fell in the mud, aged gardener was gored
on the shin, etc., but everyone very cheerful, and
in the end the cow fell down too, and was pinioned
to a log. When the animal has gone to the pound,
the next stage is the arrival of the owner, always a
poor man and in tears. When a rich man's cow is
caught, he hires a poor man to cry for him. I am in-
exorable, not through strength of mind, but because
it seems idle to be otherwise. So many cows come and
eat so many of our few plants, and what is the use of
thrice proclaiming through Dewas, by torchlight and
to the sound of drums, that cows will be punished,
if one excuses them?*

Meanwhile a political problem had developed up
at Mussoorie, where Vikky, aged eleven, was staying,
and where the Maharajah of Dewas Junior, aged about
fifty, had also arrived. Unable to cope with the crisis,
Vikky's Indian tutor despatched on June 3rd the following appeal for guidance.

May it please Your Highness:

As His Highness Junior has become the member of the Happy Valley club and the dear prince is the member of the same club, so we daily meet each other and sometime play tennis too.

I have already requested to send me instructions And I most humbly and respectfully beg to request Your Highness to be please enough to order me how to deal with His Highness Junior.

Yesterday His Highness Junior asked the dear prince to see the English theatre with him but as I have no instructions I was obliged to ask the prince to send a slip to his English governess, and so a slip was sent to her, enquiring what to answer Him. She came herself and saw Him and accepted the invitation, and so the dear prince will be going with me at four o'clock tomorrow to see the theatre with His Highness Junior.

Though I am all the time with dear prince and he is not a moment alone (but I must have instruction in such cases).

There is another prince, from Bengal, he is also the member of the Happy Valley Club, and is of nearly twelve, so being of the same age they do play tennis and other games together (but never alone).

The health of dear prince is improving, the companions are also improving in their health.

H.H. was suspicious of Junior Branch on principle, and discouraged me from calling at his court ("He would not know how to receive you properly"). So the tutor's problem must have seemed to him a real one. On the other hand he did not take any consistent interest in his son and the appeal remained unanswered.

❧ THE INSULT ❧

There is now a gap of almost a month in my Dewas letters. I was away at Hyderabad with Masood. On my return I resume fortissimo:

July 20th
We are in a funny whirl. I have been Insulted, but you are not going to be as angry as you expect, for it was an official insult. The Agent to the Governor General for Central India came in state to visit us and, according to custom, H.H. calls on him first at the Guest House. Whole programme arranged beforehand—how many steps everyone is to advance, and

all the rest of it. Down we went and sat in a row in A.G.G.'s tent, we on one side and they opposite. Attar and pan were then distributed to our side by the other—the usual ceremonial.

There had already been talks between H.H. and Colonel Adams, the P.A., as to whether I should receive these ingredients from A.G.G.'s chief of staff (who is English) or from his Indian attaché, H.H. wishing for former, but saying latter would not offend him. Moment comes. Chief of staff works down line and stops above me. I resign myself without too much of a shock to receiving from Indian and get ready handkerchief for the scent. P.A. opposite begins genial but anxious motions towards me with his hands. A.G.G. holds H.H. in close converse. When Indian attaché takes up his duties, it is below me so that I am excluded from the honours altogether. What this means in an Indian court you can't imagine, and I could scarcely. I merely felt a little flat.

As soon as our procession returned to the Palace, I mentioned it to H.H., who grew livid with passion —partly, and I know largely, for my sake, but partly for his own, because the omission implied that the A.G.G. would not recognise his right to have Europeans under him. Since the Government of India has recognised my appointment, it does seem absurd. The upshot of the Insult was that I had a very pleasant time with nothing to do.

I was at once forbidden to dance attendance on the visitors, and the printed programme was drastically altered. In due course my absence was remarked. "Where is Mr. Forster?" asks the P.A. at the tennis party, to which H.H. replies: "I am not sure whether he will come. He is rather out of spirits." Glances between P.A. and A.G.G.

When Mr. Forster does come, H.H. rises, leaves company and greets him effusively. I sit down far away from officials. P.A. and chief of staff seek me out with remarks about weather. But the A.G.G. remains aloof and glares—an elderly colonel. Official banquet in evening. Icy speeches on both sides. Subtle expressions of annoyance and contempt from H.H.

By this time I was annoyed myself—the surrounding atmosphere engendered it, and when half the company is violently upholding you against the remainder, you become self-conscious. So when A.G.G., who had ignored me the whole day, held out his hand after the cinema, I bowed stiffly, and grasped it not until it was held out a second time.

A.G.G. went. P.A. remains (unofficially) and is still here, profuse in unofficial regrets. But this is not to suffice. Our Prime Minister is to draft a protest which will go to A.G.G., and if he ignores it, to the Government of India.

Meanwhile it has rained, and saved our crops. All was prosperous in South India, but here the case grew desperate.

Our little sacred hill, generally so brown and sulky, is painted pale green now, and yesterday was a lovely sight, for there was a great popular festivity—people in bright dresses going up and down the winding paths all day. At the foot of the hill men wrestled, resembling Greek statues in so far as they wore no clothes. Most were rather ugly, but one or two beautifully formed, and their savage cries, and the sunlit hill above them, and the scarlet groups of women on its slopes, and the temple on the summit thronged with worshippers, and the elephants with freshly painted faces—well, it was all very nice.

We went up on an elephant—P.A., wife, daughter and self, took off our shoes, made an offering to the Goddess (youngest and most amiable of seven sisters, but I should not like to meet her on a dark night) and returned on foot, buying some toys—straddly black horses, but they will be difficult to pack.

The Insult rumbled on for some weeks. That same evening Colonel Adams indited to the Maharajah a letter from the Guest House. It is a strange letter: for one thing he has omitted to sign it—Freud may have intervened. Beautifully typed, bound with purple ribbon, stamped "Political Agent in Malwa" around a lion and unicorn in blue, it contains such sentences as, "I understood you to say that you had no feeling one way or the other whether Mr. Forster should receive itr and pan or no, and I so represented it to Colonel Jones, who decided, that as in his opinion there was room for doubt whether Mr. Forster, as an European on Your Highness' staff, should receive itr and pan at all, it would be better, as Your Highness had (as I understood) no strong feeling in the matter, it would be better that he should not receive it at least until the question had been settled." Such a sentence could neither clarify nor conciliate. We held our heads high and appealed unto Simla.

In Dewas the Insult advantaged me. My colleagues rallied round me because I had suffered on their behalf. They had always been courteous: now there was marked consideration and some display of affection. I felt this again at Nagpur later on, where, as an Englishman on an elephant, I was mocked at by supporters of Swaraj: "We are very sorry indeed that you should have been exposed to this while in our company," the Dewan said. On the whole, they liked me. Some of them were jealous of my access to the throne, others were bored at seeing the same Englishman for so long. But my enemies (and I had some) were not virulent or numerous.

Another episode occurs to me in this connection. I was travelling with a few of the nobles by train— I forget where or for what purpose. We had to change at a junction and all went to dine in the restaurant. Seeing "beef" on the menu, I ordered it, as it would be a change. The waiter said "beef" was off, so I had something else, and thought no more. But a fortnight later, back in Dewas, the Maharajah said to me with great gentleness: "Morgan, I want to speak to you on a very serious subject indeed. When you were travelling with my people you asked to eat something—the name of which I cannot even mention. If the waiter had brought it, they would all have had to leave the table. So they spoke to him behind your back, and told him to tell you that it was not there. They did this because they knew you did not intend anything wrong, and because they love you."

July 28th

Yes, I love H.H. and he me, and I am glad to have had this extraordinary experience, but it has been disappointing to be given so little that I can do and so much that I cannot. Not that he feels I have been a failure. If Colonel Wilson returns (and I think now that he will) it will be in the autumn, and I shall leave then. If he settles not to return, I have suggested leaving in September, after the Simla visit, but I fear H.H. will want me to see him through the Prince of Wales too. Which means I shall see about 50,000 rupees spent.

I must write a sample day another day—yesterday was partly occupied by a boat—a dinghy—the last of our unnecessary expenses I hope, for H.H. really is alarmed at last. The boat, having broken one bullock cart, and been held up by floods at the Sipra, reached us and now lies in the tennis pavilion!

I am sorry the sari daunts you. Cut off the ends! They are lovely when put on but very difficult to drape and tie—only an Indian servant can do it. H.H. was so pleased with your card and so sweet. He said: "I liked it all except the first two words, and I know that it was you who wrote those." I said, "But what was my mother to call you, if not Your Highness?" He replied, "She could have begun, Dear Morgan's Friend."

GOKUL ASHTAMI

The following letters on the Gokul Ashtami Festival are the most important of my letters home, for they describe (if too facetiously) rites in which a European can seldom have shared.

August 3rd

This month is to be devoted, not to say abandoned, to religion, and we move down to the Old Palace in the heart of the town, to be stung by mosquitoes and bitten by bugs. I have already helped to choose the

"Lord of the Universe" some new clothes. He is fortunately only six inches high, but he had to have eight suits, and he has several companions who must also be dressed, and the bill for this alone will be not far short of £30. The costume is simple in its cut—two bell-shaped pieces joined by two tabs, the doll's head going through the hole between the tabs and the stuff hanging in front and behind. Each suit is embroidered with pearls. There is also an outer garment, hanging negligee fashion over the shoulders.

We went down to the Old Palace the other day for a preliminary canter. At the end of the long narrow temple hall stood the Dewan with a wreath of roses round his neck, singing, and supported by the Doctor, the Minister of Public Works, and other notables. They faced the shrine, which was at the other end and looked like a flower show on the last day, just before the people come to take away their exhibits. Dolly was there, smothered in the rubbish, lost in the scuffle in fact; and the hall itself, which has architectural beauty, was likewise smothered in mess and appallingness. I squatted against one of the pillars, occasionally smiling at the singers, which seemed the proper thing to do. I wonder what it is all about. It

is certainly the most important thing in these people's lives. His Highness will also sing. Electric light
(£100 this) will be specially installed, and Dolly must
also have a new bed and a new mosquito net.

August 10th

No news, except of a most local nature. Religion ap-
proaches, to me in a very tangible form, as I have been
hit on the head by an iron bar belonging to a sacred
swing. Ladies and children like to swing at this season,
and although our palace is so modern there are rings
in the drawing-room ceiling on which the apparatus
can be fixed. We hung the bars up—they take the
place of ropes, so imagine their length—and then one
of our half-witted menials brightly lifted one of them
from below so that the hook came out of the ring. I
was not the least hurt—a miracle why. My skull must
be pretty thick. His Highness was horrified and trans-
fixed, and began massaging my head, which did not
seem the proper treatment to me. A car rushed off
for the doctor—but nothing wrong, no pain either at
the time or afterwards, the menial was fined two rupees and there it ended.

Collision with this holy article seems to have made

me active. *I have dismissed Kanaya, the cleverest and wickedest of our drivers—had him up in the car and took it from him before he could know where he was and could consequently make hash of the machinery. But the immediate effects were awful. The man whom I expected to replace him couldn't manage the car, and Malarao and myself, who thought we would go a quiet evening drive, were brought to a standstill six miles out of Dewas and had to walk back. We sent out petrol—said to be the trouble—but at 10 P.M. car hadn't returned, so I had to go out in other car. That stuck too. Lovely fireflies, but they did not do instead. At last we reached the first car—it wouldn't move. We wobbled back to Dewas for rope—that too no good and we had to leave the car on the road for the night, I not to bed till 3 A.M. It was dragged in by bullocks on the morrow. I was in despair, and thought Kanaya had managed to get at our cars after all, but it proves to be no more than dirt in the works, and they are going now and I have found another driver.*

Weather cool, and there is abundance of rain. Our Tank is filling at last, and we are going to launch the boat on it today, if it doesn't rain.

August 17th

The weather keeps cool, cloudy and rainy: the best monsoon for years, the crops in perfect condition, and everyone happy. The feast begins Thursday. I have been bothered over the electric lighting for the Old Palace which has to be temporarily installed. We gave the job to the Indore state people, as they have a competent English superintendent, with the result that our own people, when he asked them for a bucket and an axe, said that they had not any, and that he had contracted to do the business and must fetch a bucket from Indore. I don't think it was malice on their part, for they want the electric light so they may sing hymns all night as well as all day. They were just too silly to co-operate. I have not seen much of them yet, I mean of the Old Palace officials. They are a strange and aged company. We go down on Thursday, and I expect an interesting if uncomfortable time. For ten days nothing may be killed, not even an egg. This happens all through the state. But animals that have been killed already—i.e., tinned food —I may consume provided I come up to the New Palace to do so. No shoes can be worn in the O.P. I must either go barefoot or ruin my socks.

Colonel Wilson tells me he will be out in the middle of October, but it is all rather queer, for he does not mention a date to H.H. Indeed he is more than rather queer, I fancy. He had a railway accident last year, and he is not young, and though his letters to me are pleasant, those to H.H. are full of bitter accusations against everyone and everything. There is certain to be tension between him and myself, and H.H. realises this and will arrange that we meet in Bombay, not at Dewas; which will ease the situation.

Last week I went for the day to Sarangpore, one of our provincial capitals, which is embedded in a part of Gwalior state and distant over fifty miles from us. A melancholy and deserted town, beautifully placed on a hill above the Kali Sind river, through whose waters we had to motor. We went because there was a famous dacoit in the jail there, and it was feared he would shake it down and run away. He was transferred to the officers of a neighbouring state who claimed him under an extradition treaty. The jail, like every other public office, was round a courtyard, and the prisoners peeped through the flimsy bars and took an interest in all that went on—all except the dacoit who feigned to be prostrate with dysentery.

Across the road was another courtyard, a huge mosque now ruinous. The whole town was in the last stage of decay, houses nodding, lakes of water in the main street, and in the hospital nothing and nobody except a little tame fawn which skipped up and down in the dispensary. There was once a weaving industry at Sarangpore, but everything has ended, or is ending, and the inhabitants seemed only to have stayed because they had forgotten to go away.

Sarangpore—it received its name from Sarang Singh in the thirteenth century—was our second most important city. For a short time it had become a capital for the Junior Branch. It had had a distinguished past. The Rajput poetess and heroine Rup Mati killed herself here, and here the Emperor Akbar was detained by floods. So almost were we. On our homeward journey the car was loaded up with bags of rupees—tribute badly needed in the capital—and it stuck in the middle of the Kali Sind ford. We were nearly overwhelmed, and our treasure with us. Science prevailed, after some agitated gruntings, and that was my last of Sarangpore.

Our other provincial centre, Alot, I never visited.

It caused us some anxiety, for it had a railway station in Junior Branch territory, and the disciples of Gandhi used to alight there and shout subversive slogans at us over the border.

Old Palace
August 24th

This ought to be an interesting letter. It is the fourth day of the festival and I am getting along all right, though I collapsed at first. The noise is so appalling. Hymns are sung to the altar downstairs without ceasing. The singers, in groups of eight, accompany themselves on cymbals and a harmonium. At the end of two hours a new group pushes in from the back. The altar has also a ritual which is independent of the singing. A great many gods are on visit and they all get up at 4:30 A.M.—they are not supposed to be asleep during the festival, which is reasonable considering the din, but to be enjoying themselves. They have a bath and are anointed and take a meal, which is over about 9 A.M. At twelve is another service, during which three bands play simultaneously in the little courtyard, two native bands and one European, affecting a merry polka, while these united strains are

pierced by an enormous curved horn, rather fine,
which is blown whenever incense is offered. And
still I am only at the beginning of the noise. Children
play games all over the place, officials shout.

Last night I had a dreadful dream about Verouka
[our cat]. I thought I had shown him a mechanical
doll that frightened him so that he went mad and
raced round and round in a room overhead. I woke
up to find it was the thudding of the old steam engine
which we have tinkered up to drive our electric light.

As I said, the noise was too much at first, but Bapu
Sahib's kindness and foresight for others never fail.
I can always retire to the Guest House which is peaceful and now very beautiful since the Tank is full, and
there is a complete staff of servants there and European food. I needn't stay here a moment longer than
I like.

Well, what's it all about? It's called Gokul Ashtami
—i.e., the eight days feast in honour of Krishna who
was born at Gokul near Muttra, and I cannot yet discover how much of it is traditional and how much
due to H.H. What troubles me is that every detail,
almost without exception, is fatuous and in bad taste.
The altar is a mess of little objects, stifled with rose

leaves, the walls are hung with deplorable oleographs, the chandeliers, draperies—everything bad. Only one thing is beautiful—the expression on the faces of the people as they bow to the shrine, and he himself is, as always, successful in his odd rôle. I have never seen religious ecstasy before and don't take to it more than I expected I should, but he manages not to be absurd. Whereas the other groups of singers stand quiet, he is dancing all the time, like David before the ark, jigging up and down with a happy expression on his face, and twanging a stringed instrument that hangs by a scarf round his neck. At the end of his two hours he gets wound up and begins composing poetry which is copied down by a clerk, and yesterday he flung himself flat on his face on the carpet. Ten minutes afterwards I saw him as usual, in ordinary life. He complained of indigestion but seemed normal and discussed arrangements connected with the motor cars.

I cannot see the point of this, or rather in what it differs from ordinary mundane intoxication. I suppose that if you believe your drunkenness proceeds from God it becomes more enjoyable. Yet I am very much muddled in my own mind about it all, for H.H. has what one understands by the religious sense and it comes out all through his life. He is always thinking of others and refusing to take advantage of his position in his dealings with them; and believing that his God acts similarly towards him.

The Old Palace is built round a courtyard about fifty feet square, the temple-hall being along one side on the ground floor. The hall is open to the court and divided into three or four aisles by thick pillars. The singers stand at one end of the chief aisle, the shrine is at the other end, red carpet between. The public squats against the pillars and is controlled, of course incompetently, by schoolboy volunteers. The heat is immense and, since H.H. disdains adventitious comforts, he has the electric fans turned off when his time comes to sing.

I don't think I can describe it better than this, and it is difficult to make vivid what seems so fatuous. There is no dignity, no taste, no form, and though I am dressed as a Hindu I shall never become one. I don't think one ought to be irritated with idolatry because one can see from the faces of the people that it touches something very deep in their hearts. But it is natural that missionaries, who think these ceremonies wrong as well as inartistic, should lose their tempers.

Next week I shall have the crisis of the festival to describe—the announcement of Krishna's birth (for he is not born yet!) and the procession from the Old Palace to the Tank, where a clay model of the village of Gokul will be thrown into the waters, and so it will end. Before I forget though, we none of us wear shoes or socks inside the Old Palace. My feet suffered at first, but they can walk over heaps of coal now, as they have to whenever the electric light goes wrong. The costume is a turban (sāfar), a long coat, and a dhoti, which last resembles a voluminous yet not entirely efficient pair of bathing drawers. I have learnt to tie my own dhoti—the turban is much more difficult and I cannot acquire the knack. If you get the dhoti too short it is not thought elegant, and if you get it too long you catch your bare foot in the folds and fall down.

My bedroom at the Old Palace is secluded (except for noise), since it is upstairs, through the Durbar Hall. This is fine—I described it in a letter eight years ago—and it is now free from mess, which has been carried below to adorn the temple, so one can see its proportions. Nothing remains in it except the gaddi, a sacred featherbed with which the fortunes of the dynasty are mysteriously connected. I am told— and I can well believe it—that some of the stuffing has been in that bed for generations. A row of little roses are placed on the bolster every day, and there are two lamps at night. H.H. comes up once in every twenty-four hours to worship the bed: except for this excursion he is forbidden to leave the ground floor of the palace. I shall never be at an end of the queer-nesses. But give every place its due. There are no smells and (as far as I can testify) no bugs. It is the noise, the noise, the noise, the noise which sucks one into a whirlpool, from which there is no re-emerging. The whole of what one understands by music seems lost for ever, or rather seems never to have existed.

I am finishing at the Guest House! The Tank looks so pretty and if it does not rain I shall take the boat out.

Guest House
August 28th

For four hours yesterday evening I walked barefoot in petticoats through the streets with black and red powders smeared over my forehead, cheeks and nose.

Things began to warm up at 11:30 P.M. on the 26th when, dressed in our best, we sat cross-legged in the temple aisles, awaiting the Birth. The altar was as usual smothered in mess and the gold and silver and rich silks that make up its equipment were so disposed as to produce no effect. Choked somewhere in rose leaves, lay chief Dolly, but I could not locate him. Why, since he had been listening to hymns for eight days, he was now to be born was a puzzle to me; but no one else asked the question, and of course the festival is no more illogical than Christmas, though it seemed so, owing to its realism. My memory is so bad and the muddle so great, that I forget the details of the Birth already, but the Maharajah announced it from his end of the carpet and then went to the altar and buried his face in the rose leaves, much moved. Next, a miniature cradle was set up in the aisle, and a piece of crimson silk, folded so that it looked like an old woman over whom a traction engine has passed, was laid in it and rocked by him, Bhau Sahib, the Dewan, the Finance Member, and other leading officials of the state. Noise, I need hardly add, never stopped—the great horn brayed, the cymbals clashed, the harmonium and drums did their best, while in the outer courtyard the three elephants were set to bellow and the band played "Nights of Gladness" as loudly as possible.

Under these circumstances the child was named "Krishna" by H.H. I was now nearly dead with the heat. What I thought were little animals running down my legs proved to be streams of sweat. But I sat while the chief personages revisited the altar and were concealed by a pink and green curtain from our gaze, behind which they ate.—I forgot to say that we were each given a paper tray of red powder and that when the Birth was announced we threw it in the air so that the whole aisle was filled with crimson smoke. Or that H.H. carried the folded silk (which did not contain the image, who mustn't be moved) in his arms among the people who squatted row behind row far into the distance. And I must not waste time telling of my troubles with the decorations, of the mottoes from English poetry that wouldn't stick up, or of the glass battery cases that I filled with water and live fish and into which some humanitarian idiot dropped handfuls of flour so that the fish should not starve. You couldn't have seen a whale. Oh, such an emptying and slopping to get it right, and two of the fish died through overeating, and had to be buried in a flowerpot in case H.H. should see them.

I must get on to the final day—the most queer and also the most enjoyable day of the series. There was a sermon in the morning, but after it we began to play games before the altar in a ceremonial fashion; there were games of this sort in the Christian Middle Ages and they still survive in the Cathedral of Seville at Easter. With a long stick in his hand H.H. churned imaginary milk and threshed imaginary wheat and hit (I suppose) imaginary enemies and then each took a pair of little sticks, painted to match the turban, and whacked them together. (You must never forget that cymbals never cease, nor does a harmonium.) Real butter came next and was stuck on the forehead of a noble in a big lump and when he tried to lick it off another noble snatched it from behind. (Very deep meaning in all this, says H.H., though few know it.) I had a little butter too. Then we went under a large black vessel, rather handsome, that was hung up in the aisle, and we banged it with our painted sticks, and the vessel broke and a mass of grain soaked in milk fell down on our heads. We fed each other with it. This was the last of the games, and the mess was now awful and swarms of flies came.

Still holding our painted sticks we went into the court and began to form the procession. There was a palanquin, large and gorgeous, and shaped like a gondola with silver dragons at each end. Dolly got in with his rose leaves and tea services and a chromo picture of Tukaram, the Maratha saint, and banana leaves and fans and the village of Gokul and I don't know what else. Still I couldn't see him. But H.H., determined I should, broke off his hymns and brought me quite close. I saw the thing at last—face like an ill-tempered pea: curious little lump for so much to centre round.

The procession started with an elephant—no one on its back, to indicate humility—then all of the army that possess uniforms or musical instruments, then the twelve bands of singers who had been at it all the week, but they showed no signs of feebleness, H.H. leading the last band, just in front of the palanquin, which another elephant followed. The view, looking back, after we had passed through the outer palace gateway, was really fine. The eighteenth-century architecture, though not splendid, is better than

1 6 7

anything Dewas has produced since—blue birds over the arch and elephants tussling on the cornice—and the rich round banners that accompanied the palanquin (shaped like magnifying-glasses) and the pennons, and the fans of peacock's feather—all under a pink evening sky.

Timed for three, the start was at six, and the pace so slow that darkness fell before the palace went out of sight. The route was kept fairly well by lines of schoolboys, who joined hands. Being barefoot, I was allowed to walk inside the lines, indeed close to the palanquin if I chose. The preacher of the sermon and another very pious man walked with me, indeed we were hand in hand, and the predominant sanctity of our group brought offerings of sugar candy and coconut in large quantities and smears of red and black powder for our foreheads and noses. I was very glad of them, the offerings I mean, as the night wore on, and the other holy men gave me theirs as well, and when I began to feel sickish we gave to children instead, and thus acquired the merit of being saints. I enjoyed the walk, for the preacher (an Indore man) was well educated and explained what the various groups were singing—some praised God without attributes, others with attributes: the same mixture of fatuity and philosophy that ran through the whole festival.

A lady fanatic was in the Dewan's group. She was gaudily yet neatly dressed in purple and yellow, a circlet of jasmine flowers was round her chignon and in her hands were a pair of tongs with which she accompanied herself. We could not discover whether she was praising God with or without attributes. Her voice was too loud. She nodded and smiled in a very pleasant way.

My feet held out well—I had hardened them purposely in the previous days until I could run over heaps of coal. But my back—I thought it would break. "We are pained to see your pain," remarked the Indore preacher, "but we are greatly pleased by your so good nature. We have not met an Englishman like you previously."

At the jail there was a great crush, for a prisoner was released—a lady who had murdered her husband, and has been pulling up weeds in the palace garden for me in consequence. Her expression was beautiful as she flung herself before H.H. and the Dewan. The expressions of most people were beautiful that day.

By ten we reached the Tank and the queer impressive ceremony of drowning the Town of Gokul was performed. The town—about a yard square—was stripped of its flagstaffs and, after prayers and meals, was handed to a man whose hereditary duty it is to drown the Town of Gokul. He was half naked and waded into the water and the darkness, pushing the city before him on a floating tray. When he was far out he upset it, all the dolls fell into the water and were seen no more, and the town, being of mud, dissolved immediately. The tray was brought back and worshipped slightly, while elephants trumpeted and cannon were fired.

I limped to a victoria which I had waiting and drove straight to the Guest House at the other side of the Tank, there to wash my face, drink sherry, eat sardines, sausages, and stewed fruit, and reel to my bed. The others had two more hours of it, getting back to the Old Palace at midnight.

As to the explanation of this, as apart from what one was told by the pious, I know too little to conjecture, but was reminded of the Adonis festival, where the God is born, dies, and is carried to the water, all in a short time. H.H. says the Town of

Gokul is meant to represent Krishna who cannot of course be drowned. His end came next morning, but my own end was too near for me to go down to the Old Palace to witness it. At midday the purple and green curtain was drawn before the altar and all the prominent officials burst into tears.

Festivals are endless. Today Ganpati (the Elephant God) has a little show, the day before yesterday the bullocks were worshipped, tomorrow ladies may eat practically nothing but vegetable marrows, and during the Gokul Ashtami itself there was a popular festival, quite unconnected with it, of which the court people knew nothing. Perhaps I will describe it another time. It was very primitive—much older than Hinduism, I am sure; really the worship of the spirit of vegetation. But by now you will have heard enough of religions of sorts. I have, and am ashamed that the good people here should have felt I was so sympathetic. The mere fact that I did not hold aloof seemed enough—they did not the least mind my saying that it all meant nothing to me.

Since beginning this letter I have distressed H.H. by suggesting that I should receive no salary after the end of this month. I said that I was not competent, *either by training or temperament, for the work I had to do here, and that the side of me that is competent was never employed. As always, he was sweet and understanding, and has promised to reform at some early, but future, date. Colonel Wilson's cable still doesn't come.*

Since attending Gokul Ashtami, I have researched a little about it. I will begin by quoting a letter which the Maharajah wrote to Malcolm right back in 1909. It is an authoritative account of the event, and it has great beauty. ("Your sister" is his wife, who was then still with him. "Your poor brother" is himself.)

As you may well imagine I was absolutely engaged in the Gokulastami Festival which I am glad to tell you passed off very well. The Festival began from the first of this month and sixth, eighth and ninth were main days and lasted till yesterday. Well, it was altogether a splendid show I think. Everybody did his duty very well. The Bhajans of Dewansahib, Rajarangi and the old Fadnis were well sung, specially it was very striking to see the Dewan singing them with his austere but devoted face and an attitude of absolute unity with the Deities in front of him.

172

Every day the hall where the Gods were enthroned was decorated by different people according to their different tastes. Public Works Department came on first day and arranged a beautiful small wooden house and a garden before the Holy Throne. Second day came the Khasgi * *and the decorations were simple but fine being done with all the different leaves and flowers from the garden and toys from the Khasgi stock. Third day came the warlike appearance to the Hall. The Sainapati brought out all the best arms and instruments from the Military Department and the lances of silver formed beautiful arches and the small guns, specially prepared for decorations by the Late Highness, formed a formidable appearance before the Holy Altar. Fourth day was superb in the decorations with finer and subtler things of life. The Dewansahib wrote out on the walls beautiful and instructive mottoes from old Holy Books and decorated the place with fine shawls, bunting, and plantain tree arches. The typewriter worked on till 9 P.M. bringing out leaflets which declared mottoes of victory to Sri Krishna God and so on.*

* Another Public Works Department.

On the fifth day your sister and Shri Bhausahib Maharaj decorated the place with rich shawls and some ornaments, and richly coloured flowers and leaves were to be found all over the walls—a fine scene. On the sixth your poor brother had to decorate the place and he did it according to his ignorant tastes. All the silver and gold ornaments and treasures were put in different places and the silver and gold lances from the military formed arches at the top of the hall and the names of the great heroes, incarnations, and religious reformers were stuck on the wall. The Throne of the God was studded with jewelry.

At 12 P.M. on the sixth the whole army fired salvoes and the guns blew forth and present arms were done. The whole hall was thronged by people and amidst the great and devoted excitement the God Krishna was born.

On the eighth was great feast in the Palace and Brahmins, Marathas and others sat to dine. Ninth was the procession to the tank. We all sang in front of the Palanquin of the God. The other days were engaged with usual worship and rites and ceremonies. There is nothing more of interest from here. Plague is increasing at Indore—we are all anxious.

Such was his account. But what did he feel when he danced like King David before the altar? What were his religous opinions?

The first question is easier to answer than the second. He felt as King David and other mystics have felt when they are in the mystic state. He presented well-known characteristics. He was convinced that he was in touch with the reality he called Krishna. And he was unconscious of the world around him. "You can come in during my observances tomorrow and see me if you like, but I shall not know that you are there," he once told Malcolm. And he didn't know. He was in an abnormal but recognisable state; psychologists have studied it.

More interesting, and more elusive, are his religious opinions. The unseen was always close to him, even when he was joking or intriguing. Red paint on a stone could evoke it. Like most people, he implied beliefs and formulated rules for behaviour, and since he had a lively mind, he was often inconsistent. It was difficult to be sure what he did believe (outside the great mystic moments) or what he thought right or wrong. Indians are even more puzzling than Westerners here. Mr. Shastri, a spiritual and subtle Brahmin, once uttered a puzzler: "If the Gods do a thing, it is a reason for men not to do it." No doubt he was in a particular religious mood. In another mood he would have urged us to imitate the Gods. And the Maharajah was all moods. They played over his face, they agitated his delicate feet and hands. To get any pronouncement from so mercurial a creature on the subject, say, of asceticism, was impossible. As a boy, he had thought of retiring from the world, and it was an ideal which he cherished throughout his life, and which, at the end, he would have done well to practise. Yet he would condemn asceticism, declare that salvation could not be reached through it, that it might be Vedantic but it was not Vedic, and matter and spirit must both be given their due. Nothing too much! In such a mood he seemed Greek.

He believed in the heart, and here we reach firmer ground. "I stand for the heart. To the dogs with the head," cries Herman Melville, and he would have agreed. Affection, or the possibility of it, quivered through everything, from Gokul Ashtami down to daily human relationships. When I returned to England and he heard that I was worried because the post-war world of the '20's would not add up into

sense, he sent me a message. "Tell him," it ran, "tell
him from me to follow his heart, and his mind will see
everything clear." The message as phrased is too fac-
ile: doors open into silliness at once. But to remember
and respect and prefer the heart, to have the instinct
which follows it wherever possible—what surer help
than that could one have through life? What better
hope of clarification? Melville goes on: "The reason
that the mass of men fear God and at bottom dislike
Him, is because they rather distrust His heart." With
that too he would have agreed.

To return to Gokul Ashtami.

It is (or was) celebrated throughout India, often
under the name of Jamnashtami—the Eight Days of
the Birth. But I have never heard of it being celebrated so sumptuously. It had been appropriated and
worked up by the Dewas dynasty. Priests took little
part in it, the devout were in direct contact with their
god, emotion meant more than ritual. This is indeed
consonant with Maratha history. There always has
been a contest between the Brahmins (who were once
powerful as Peshwas) and the dynasties that sprang
from the founder of the Maratha empire. Sivaji, a
great warrior and belonging to a low caste, believed

in bhakti, in our union with the Divine through love.
The Maharajah of Dewas, not a great warrior, believed
in it too. He maintained one side of the Maratha
tradition. In his religious conversations he spoke of
Krishna only. I do not remember him mentioning
the racial god of the Maratha people and of his own
house, Khandoba. But Khandoba, though fierce and
primitive, could also be approached through love:
Sivaji adored him and so did Sivaji's friend, the poet
Tukaram. "Tukaram, Tukaram, thou art my father
and my mother and all things" we would sing, time
after time, until we seemed to be worshipping a poet.

The literary authorities for the Krishna birth stories
are the *Bhagavad Purana*, Book X, and the *Vishnu
Purana*, Book V.

The *Bhagavad Purana*, which is the earlier in date,
describes how Kamsa, the wicked king of Muttra, was
driving his sister to her marriage when a voice warned
him that her eighth child would destroy him. He
therefore tried to kill her in the processional chariot,
but was appeased by her promise that each child
should be delivered up to him when born. So she
was married, and she and her husband kept their

promise. But their seventh child, Balarama, was transferred before birth into the womb of another wife, and the eighth child, Krishna, likewise escaped. The ninth child, a daughter, Kamsa tried to kill, but she mocked him, confirmed his doom and disappeared as a goddess into heaven. Like Herod, he then gave orders for all children in his kingdom to be massacred. Great was the lamentation, but Krishna, hidden away in the village of Gokul, was safe. He, the supreme God, the incarnation of Vishnu, grew up as a herdsman, and worked and played with country boys and girls. He also performed miracles, and in due time he went up with his brother Balarama to Muttra, to wrestle before the king. Kamsa, enraged at their victories over his champions, gave orders that their father and mother should be killed. Krishna—the moment had come—leapt at the tyrant, flung his crown from his head, and tore him asunder in the arena, as a lion tears an elephant. The text continues: "Kamsa, who had always trembled at the bottom of his heart at the thought of the Supreme Being, whether he ate or drank or walked or slept or breathed, now had the unusual honour of seeing him face to face, and of being reunited to his divinity."

If one can judge from a translation, and if one can condone silliness and prolixity, the tenth book of the *Bhagavad Purana* must be a remarkable work. It has warmth and emotion and a sort of divine reck-lessness and a sort of crude human happiness. Read-ing it today, I can trace parallels with our performance at Dewas. Krishna is "a raft to sail on," he is "as small as the footprint of a calf," he is born "at midnight, in the thickest darkness, like the full moon in the east, when all the directions were peaceful and the minds of the good and of the gods were serene." "Various and wonderful instruments of music are played when he is born," and the sportive cowboys "smear one another with butter" as we did. In in-fancy he and his brother "drag their little feet with the tinkling sounds of ornaments on them through the moist places and looked beautiful with their limbs besmeared with mire." He steals trifles, he "commits nuisance in the premise of the house," then "stands like a very quiet boy." He even eats earth and dirt: "Look in my mouth, then," he says, and "the whole Universe of mobile and immobile creatures" is seen inside it. As he grows up he goes with his friends to the fields and woods, breakfasts by a stream while the cows stray, eats while they sit around him, "his flute between his belly and his garment, the soft morsel in the left hand and fruits between his fingers, walled in by his comrades, and laughing and making them laugh." "He, the one deity of all sacrifices, exhibiting the gaiety of lads, while the celestial world looked on." "Thy glory purifies all the world," sing the bees. They dance, sing, fight, imitate birds and animals, and when he is tired he "goes beneath a tree and rests on beds of tender leaves, with his head cushioned on a herds-boy's thigh." The frivolity, triviality goes on, and every now and then it cracks, as at our festival, and discloses depths. "What am I," cries the poet, "invested with a body of seven spans in a small part of this egg, the world? How inconceivably vast is the glory of Thee, of whom a pore is like a window through which innumerable eggs of Universes pass to and fro like atoms?" When the festival was over one was left with something inexplicable, which grows a little clearer with the passage of the years. One was left, too, aware of a gap in Christianity: the canonical gospels do not record that Christ laughed or played. Can a man be perfect if he never laughs or plays? Krishna's jokes may be vapid, but they bridge a gap.

This is not the only Krishna rite that I have witnessed. At Chhatarpur, in Bundelkhand, delightful tableaux and dances were staged for the benefit of its exotic Maharajah: Lowes Dickinson has described them in his *Appearances*, and J. R. Ackerly in his *Hindu Holiday*. But they were purely personal: no tradition upheld them.

⚜ ON TOUR ⚜

New Palace
September 2nd
Next week His Highness, His Highness' brother, the Chief Secretary, the Private Secretary, the Assistant Private Secretary, His Highness' brother's two Secretaries, the Prime Minister, the Minister of Public Works, old Mr. Kadam, Ambunana the Priest, and fourteen servants set out for Nagpur, in British India. It is a Maratha Educational Conference.

It is perfect weather for the crops and everyone is happy, including the Treasury officials who hope to fill their depleted coffers. But I find the gloom and

the low clouds and the very green earth rather depress-
ing, the more so since the Palace is built to exclude
light. During much of the day it is too dark to read.
The bullocks were worshipped yesterday, their horns
were painted red and green for the occasion, but they
had a very damp outing, and the little mud bullocks
that were placed ceremonially in the courtyard were
so clammy and floppy that they could scarcely stand
up.

We are for the moment leading our normal lives.
Our great festival is over and the Dowager Maharani
is back from Gwalior, also from a festival. She arrived
in some agitation—had been well received but in an
unlucky moment had been persuaded to go in a motor
boat, "a nicely boat," together with the Maharani of
Gwalior, the Maharani of Dhar and other elite. The
boat hit a rock. "The driver cry No harm Meesis," but
it was no good crying no harm, for all the Maharanis
fell on the floor. "I row a boat very nicely myself when
young, but now never. I tremble."

She explained with her usual felicity why the boat
had hit the rock. It was because she had taken part
in the festival of Ganpati, the elephant god, and had

launched a little image of him to float on the waters. Since she had gone to Gwalior in order to take part in the festival, and since it is lucky to make a Ganpati float, the mystery did but deepen. "Yes, but not lucky for my branch of the family, that is the difference. Whenever I float Ganpati, a disaster. One year I float and what next? My brother-in-law nearly breaks his arm. This time I refuse. But Her Highness the Junior Maharani begs, Her Highness Maharani of Dahr begs. I give way. I wish to give pleasure. I say Very well, I make little Ganpati float too. And you see." Scindhia revived the ladies with brandy on their arrival, his usual remedy.

To Mrs. Barger:

September 5th

It is India and 3 P.M. but so dark that I can scarcely see to write and not at all to find your letter. I go off on the royal progress tomorrow.

I tap about over this place and wonder whether I grow deaf or whether there really is no echo. Except in the direction of religion, where I allow them much, these people don't seem to move towards anything

1 8 4

important; there is no art, the literature is racial and I suspect its value; there is no intellectual interest, although His Highness at least has an excellent intellect. The music—some singers are good but most that I have heard are not, and all become bawdy at the least encouragement. It is a great misfortune for art to be associated with prostitution, not for moral reasons but because every flight of beauty or fancy is apt to be cut short. H.H. leads a "good" life as it is called, and our singing parties at the Palace are only a debauch to the superficial observer. But there is much verbal and histrionic indecency which amused me at first, not now, because I see that it takes the place of so much that I value. I am afraid that Indian singing is doomed for this reason, because all the reformers and Westernisers will have none of it. And it is, or has been, a great art.

Night has fallen, and our excellent electric light has enabled me to find your letter.

The following letters to my mother describe the tour, rather confusedly. I accompanied the court to Nagpur and Simla, left it to stay with an English friend at Agra, and with another old friend the

Maharajah of Chhatarpur, returned to Dewas, and departed again almost immediately for Dhar.

It must have been on this tour that a mirthful railway incident occurred. I arrived at the station, wherever it was, soon before our train left and found that owing to familiar mismanagement the Ruler and all his suite had been crammed into a single second-class compartment. Their luggage was with them, so that he was walled up between boxes and bundles, a god in a shrine, his legs being folded underneath him. He peeped out in the highest of spirits. "I can travel like this, I can do anything; but for you, Morgan, we have naturally been able to reserve a berth in a first." Protests were useless and he skipped out to install me. The only other passenger in the first was an army chaplain who had been pig-sticking and was rather like a pig. He surveyed me and the vociferous native with hostility. When we were alone, and the train had started on its all-night journey, I felt I ought to be easy and friendly, so I said to the chaplain, "It looks as if we are going to have the carriage to ourselves." He closed his little eyes and said, "Apparently," and we spoke no more.

Peliti's Mall Hotel,
Simla
September 19th

Such an interesting and crowded ten days. I have not
put pen to paper during them, at least in the letter-
writing way. It has been a whirl of railway journeys
and interviews, intermixed with a little work. To
begin with, the Maharajah is so pleased that you
wanted vengeance for my treatment by the A.G.G.
"Mother is perfectly right," he said. He spoke about
it to Sir John Wood, Political Secretary here. It seems
that the A.G.G. had not only been rude but grossly
disobedient. The Government of India had issued an
order to the effect that: If a native ruler had a European in his service and if the ruler and the European
both wished it, then the European was to receive the
usual courtesies from the A.G.G. at any ceremonial,
and was to receive them from a British officer: exactly
what H.H. had wanted and had been told he could
not have. The trouble is that that particular A.G.G.
has retired since the incident. He took the opportunity to be insolent, knowing that he could not be
punished for it. So there is no getting at him. What
will happen is that the P.A. will be instructed officially

1 8 7

to apologise to us both, and that the new A.G.G. will be informed of his predecessor's blunder and told not to imitate it.

I have so much to tell. It quite oppresses me. This morning Sir John (he has been very kind) got us tickets for the meeting of the Legislative Council. This afternoon H.H. had his interview with the Viceroy—a disappointment on the whole. He found him clever, but shifty and quite without charm, and he has never even asked him to dinner, which is rude considering he has come all these hundreds of miles by appointment to see him. It is said that he is most remiss socially and there is great dissatisfaction with him in Simla, although Lady Reading is popular. So here is first-hand gossip about high circles! He meant to be nice to H.H.—it wasn't that—and he will probably come and open the absurd constitution that is being inaugurated at Dewas next year.

Simla is less lovely than I remember it, because the clouds are down and the snows invisible in consequence. But it is very, very lovely all the same and has made me feel so well and energetic. Bidwai and I rose at 6:30 the other morning and went for a three hours' walk. Such glorious trees and so many ferns

and wild flowers clinging to the cliffs and lurking in
the grass and dahlias turning into creepers. We never
see a wild flower in the plains. The country becomes
green and that is all. Simla itself—i.e., the houses—is
deplorable, but the scale of the landscape is so vast
that one can lose them easily.

Now all this time I have never mentioned Nagpur,
a really extraordinary experience. Perhaps I had better
leave it for another letter. We went there to a
Maratha Educational Conference. Nagpur is British
India—capital of the Central Provinces. But it was
once a Maratha state, and two preposterous creatures
called rajahs still live there in semi-royal state. H.H.
—misguided creature—moved by patriotism and pity,
is scheming to set them on their feet again, and to
get them, not indeed Nagpur itself, but certain dis-
tricts round it which will be re-created into a native
state and abundantly misgoverned in consequence.
Of the success of his schemes I will write in another
letter. It has all been exciting but grotesque.

I met the second rajah first, and thought there
could not be a more ridiculous figure, but there was,
and it was the first rajah who is very short and fat and
dressed in cloth of gold. He has bandy legs, dyed

moustachios, and an immense flat nose covered with pink and purple pimples. A gorgeous Maratha head-dress completes the picture.

We entered the city of Nagpur on elephants, and there were camels also and riderless horses draped in costly stuff. It was a pathetic pageant, and under our feet were crowds of the Nagpur people, the most fanatical and anti-British in India, all contemptuous or indifferent, and many of them wearing the white Gandhi cap. British officials met H.H. at the station and the fort fired his salute of fifteen guns which pleased him. We gave an immense and not unsuccessful garden party. He praised my arrangements for it, and when the guests were going and I brought him some garlands for them he turned round and garlanded me instead.

I like my new servant, Hassan. He has no head and scarcely any body but is gentle and industrious and never makes difficulties. Baldeo was delighted not to come, and very polite and assiduous in instructing Hassan as to his duties. He is having an operation in the Dewas hospital in my absence, so perhaps it will leave him less grim. Our other servants are a crew. H.H. has brought his head servant, who is dirty, unshaven, idle and impertinent. Also Shankar, to act as barber for our party. Shankar is pleasant but mad, and rushes about with open razors in his hand. Then the Dewan has a servant who is also filthy dirty and also mad, but not in the same way as Shankar, adopting the maundering method. He got into my bedroom at 5:30 A.M. I leapt out of sleep and rushed at him thinking he was a thief, and he fled. It seems that he mistook my room for his master's. Finally there is Hassan, no thicker than a piece of paper, and the whole lot of them have coughs, owing to the cold. They get into our rooms when we are away and lie before the fires, which is well enough, but smoke abominable little pipes too, which is not so well.

Now it pours with rain and the porters who carry the luggage to Simla station on their heads, squat in the hotel passages, waiting for a break. We go in rickshaws, overrated and indeed detestable conveyances. Four men (who have never washed since birth owing to the cold) pull and push you at a snail's pace. No one walks at your side, because it is degrading, and you cannot talk to the inmates of the other rickshaws because they are too far away.

Guest House,
Chhatarpur,
Bundelkhand
September 26th

H.H. has asked Colonel Wilson back out of pity and because they like each other, but it is a tiresome and inconsiderate affection on the Colonel's side. We still don't know whether he will come. The Prince of Wales does not come—only to Indore where he stops three days in February and receives the chiefs of the district. So there is no question of my staying for that. Our constitution is a more dangerous trap, since Lord Reading has half promised to open it.

We left Simla on the 19th (I think it was) and I parted with the rest in the middle of the night, arriving at Agra the following midday in torrents of rain, sky black as night, not a breath of wind, earth a lake. It continued thus most of my stay, but I "managed" as people piously say, "to enjoy myself," and R. B. Smith was most hospitable and thoughtful.

After nine years, I revisited the Taj. The first time, he (or she) looked hideous and hard, but we drove down again one evening and I have never seen the vision lovelier. I went up the left-hand further minaret, and saw all the magnificent buildings glowing beneath me and all the country steaming beneath a dim red and grey sky, and just as I thought nothing could be more beautiful a muezzin with a most glorious voice gave the evening call to prayer from a mosque. "There is no God but God." I do like Islam, though I have had to come through Hinduism to discover it. After all the mess and profusion and confusion of Gokul Ashtami, where nothing ever stopped or need ever have begun, it was like standing on a mountain.

Meanwhile, more cordial telegrams dropped in from this little king, and the rain rained itself out, and I arrived here at midnight on the 24th. Hassan arrived too, though not through any effort of his own, for when the train reached Harpalpur he was asleep and nowhere to be found. They did not start until he was woken. Then he fell asleep again in the car, and almost out of it. At 2 A.M. we reached this Guest House and I ate a heavy meal. A soldier with a spear arrived with a most friendly note from the Maharajah of Chhatarpur saying that he would call on me at six next morning.

Well, it was next morning; however, I lay down, and he seemed with me in a twinkling, uglier than ever, very cordial, and sorry to childishness that I could not be his Private Secretary. We got on well, and I shine as I could not when Lowes Dickinson and Bob Trevelyan were here. He is a nice creature, but weak and exasperating and not to be lived with easily. His baby is a boy—we go out to see him tomorrow. Today we visited English people at Nowgong, an unnecessary and somewhat undignified trail. But the scenery is more glorious than words can describe. After the rains the tropical jungles are magnificent. They stretch up to the road, and though there are few flowers the slopes of the hills are covered with butterflies by day and with fireflies by night, and rabbits and peacocks are thick, and monkeys swing about. How I wish that Dewas wasn't so meagre! though I have no doubt as to which state I would choose to live in.

For one hour Hassan, two other men and two boys, have been trying to light the lamps. I write on, first at one, and when it pops out, at another. It was exactly the same here eight years ago. But I must say that on the whole this Guest House is well run, better than ours. So it ought to be, for the staff is bigger and they even have a special clerk.

The Maharajah of Chhatarpur, who always wanted what anyone else had got and tired of it when he got it, had been much upset when he heard that I had come out as Private Secretary to a rival monarch. He wrote instantly, in order to make me break my contract, and offered me twice my salary, whatever that might be. When I refused he was cross and, indeed, throughout my week's visit my stock rose and fell capriciously.

It was curious being with him after experiences of another Indian state. Chhatarpur was wilder, smaller and weaker than Dewas, and far more picturesque. Hidden away in the jungles, it is indeed one of the most romantic places I have ever seen. The Guest House stood on a steep ridge close outside the city and, as the morning mists thinned, the spires of Hindu and Jain temples appeared through the white and the treetops resembled green cushions. Beyond the city were hills. Monkeys scampered up and down the slope—black-faced because they had not helped Rama in his wars—tigers and leopards were near. No industries. No railways. Agriculture as usual, but more diversified; for instance, betel leaf was cultivated— delicate creepers twined round strings in a wattled enclosure. And there was wonderful sightseeing: the great temple group at Khajraho, which is one of the glories of India, and nearer at hand the lyrical beauties of Mau.

Mau is a half-ruined palace by the side of a lake. One passes through a pillared hall onto a terrace, and the water is reached by steps at the roots of a great tree. The water is full of growth but clear, and when the sun sets duck fly over and hundreds of fowl beat the surface with their wings, far away, making thunder. On the further side are tombs: a nymph haunts one of them; she used to eat lotus and walk on the lotus leaves. The Maharajah told me this and much more: once he brought a sorcerer to Mau to make the walls speak by some incense, but the man was a "quake," he forgot the incense and the walls have never spoken.

He was a most unusual character—mystical, and sensual, silly and shrewd. I do not think he misgoverned his kingdom, as my friend did his. He had not the energy for that. He merely omitted to govern it, and did what the English told him, lamenting or tittering all the time. He had the vaguest attitude to external affairs: a pilgrimage to Benares was the great world, so far as he was concerned. He concentrated on his health, on philosophy and religion and on his troupe of Krishna dancers, when he had one. People laughed at him and sponged on him and he knew it and laughed at them. He was exasperating, undignified, unreliable, but endearing, and there must be many who are grateful for his friendship, and regret his death. India will certainly never look upon his like again.

While with him I wrote a long chronicle letter to Lowes Dickinson, who had been my fellow guest nine years before. Here are some edited extracts. I did not post the letter locally, for it would certainly have been opened and might never have reached its destination.

Guest House,
Chhatarpur,
Bundelkhand
September 25th-October 1st
You cannot imagine what aesthetic peace I am finding here. The sense of beauty, which Dewas daily outrages, is soothed by every turn of the architecture, every clean floor and whitewashed wall. It is like

those first ten minutes after a toothache has stopped. This morning the hills, rocks, grass, crops, sky, tanks are all larger and brighter than we remember, and in every direction I see delicate ruined shrines and graceful trees. Poor little Dewas, thou are wretched scenically. Yet this is not a place to settle in. It is unlikely I shall ever see it again, and Gandhi would wipe it far more thoroughly than any Political Agent.

The Maharajah's chief problem at this minute is the finding of an English Private Secretary, and he is keener than ever because Dewas has secured one in me. Having been greatly struck by a character named Olaf in a novel by Sir Rider Haggard, he wrote to the author, asking him to send him someone as near like Olaf as possible. Sir Rider succeeded in doing this, but the Olaf could not start, owing to family reasons, and a second selection is deemed less promising.

When he comes up to the Guest House much time is spent in sending down by car to the Palace for correspondence on the secretarial crisis, or for all that has not been lost from a correspondence that he has had with Bertrand Russell on philosophy. Russell's advice, dated now from Overstrand Mansions, now from Garsington, now from Bloomsbury, made curious reading in this clime. He was helpful but firm—regretted that he had not read G. H. Lewes but believed him to be inferior to Herbert Spencer—denied that the universe has any consideration for man, but equally denied to man the right to neglect his own hopes and ideals, since this would be "to bow before an alien power." He left the Maharajah in a tight hole in fact. But every Indian hole has at least two exits, and consequently nothing anybody writes can either assist or obstruct. We have also spoken of your books, and I learn that The Magic Flute expresses very clearly your pragmatic notions as to the value of truth, and indeed that you are a pragmatist. It is a comfort to have got you pinned. Since you, some works on psychoanalysis have arrived, but they have not been apprehended yet.

The social and political situation seems much as it was. The old anxiety over the P.A. survives. The theosophist whom we knew and rather liked ended his quest for the All by falling out of a railway train. His successor is of a tougher type, says, "So you're a philosopher, Maharajah! Then you think I'm a fool and I think you're a fool."—"What reply can be made?" reflects the Maharajah mildly. He need not tolerate such impudence now that the Government of India has changed its policy. Dewas doesn't, and I am urging this monarch to kick too. He won't of course. He has even been bullied into dismissing all his actors and dancers and there are no more of those lovely Krishna performances at the Palace.

But my regrets were premature. The journal continues:

I have just driven to the Khajraho temples with the last of the Krishnas. What experiences! Why, the very existence of such a person was unknown to me until the previous evening. A chance question revealed him, and the Maharajah's idea now is that I should see as much of him as possible. We talked the whole time—I cannot think of what, since we don't know each other's languages. Intelligent and forthcoming, but the face is melancholy and possibly cruel. He sat wedged between us, a slender sphinx. I hear his acting and singing were not good, but he must have looked striking and when we got back he played to us sweetly on the flute. All the other Krishnas, all the Radhas, and all the Gopis have been swept away to appease the Government's demand for economy. This is the sole surviving protest.

September 28. Today began pleasantly enough with Krishna coming up to call upon me in diamond earrings and upon a horse that he could not ride. He was friendly and simple. But after he left, the Maharajah arrived in his most tiresome and tiring mood, worrying not on and on but round and round about his fears and plans and forebodings and whether his English secretary, when he does get one, will be faithful in twenty years' time and educate his son and heir properly. This lasted two and one half hours—I was exanimate—we drove to Mau—lovelier than ever, but I annoyed him by refusing to answer some little question that involved someone else, and he had a spurtlet of temper and said I was not his friend. Then the P.A. and party drove up and took charge—Mau is their favourite picnic site—a sumptuous tea was devoured by the English people while the Maharajah sat apart and asked permission for his Dewan to sit down—feeble and undignified move—and worried the ladies to admire his pony-hair coat.

Our drive back was no better, for a woodpecker cried from a tree on the left, and shuddering at the omen he plucked the whole of the carriage rug away from me and wrapped himself up in it. Worse—when we reached the Guest House, he made me walk up the slope to it instead of driving me to the door. This doesn't do in India, you know, it doesn't do!!! It would never have happened at Dewas. It has made me decide to go tomorrow unless warmly pressed, and I've written a note to that effect.

So the day which began so brightly has ended in mild cloud, and Krishna is to be punished for calling on me with a horse and earrings. He was told to walk quietly up, avoiding ostentation, because as soon as there is talk he may have to go and with him will depart the last channel for visions of the Deity. It will mean a closing down of the religious life. "Has he any friends of his own age?" I enquired. The answer, given with great satisfaction, was "None."

October 1st. Here I still am—quite popular again. Yesterday, after my usual early visit from royalty, I walked to the Temple of Ram-whose-hands-reach-to-his-knees, not to be confused with the Temple of the Monkey God (Hanuman-who-knocks-down-Europeans) which is close to the Guest House. H.H. continued to look in throughout the day, affectionate

but making a great caboodle about admitting me to
his palace. I have never been into the court where
we used to sit, nor even down the entrance hall: only
to the library rooms in the gallery to the left, and to
a small court at the back. Perhaps the Brahmins for-
bid it. They are powerful and are eating endlessly
meals off banana leaves.

He now says I am a "wizard" and implores me to
open my heart so that God may fill it and him, and
inspire me to relate the future. "Where are Socrates
and Plato? We do not know—yes, yes." And then
came a queer impressive story of a holy man who died
about fifty years ago and whose body could be heard
humming "Ram Ram" when you placed your ear
against it. He was dressed in women's garments to be
the bride of God and adorned with Tulsi plant, and
he was encased in a beautiful box to float down the
Ganges. But a fisherman saw the box and broke it
open, and finding only a corpse inside flung it on
the bank, and jackals ate it, and that was the end of
that holy man.

Carriage promised for evening to take me down to
the Palace and some singing. Then a note, "I don't
feel fit," then the carriage after all, into which, mainly

out of curiosity, I got. We sat in the back entrance, with Krishna and Radha opposite us on little low-legged chairs. They looked bored. Musicians came and a few Brahmins, and there was one boy who danced religiously in short red skirt and pale blue shawl (sari of sorts). He was good. Everyone had had a bath and was in a state of untouchability which renders the atmosphere chill. Radha's presence, if you have managed to read all this letter, may surprise you. It did me. A lie, I have been told a lie. The troupe of dancers remain here after all. I railed H.H. on his deceit. He was all merriment, and laughed into his sleeve.

I expect to get off today, since my luggage has gone, but it has been a great difficulty—tires burst, drivers sicken mysteriously. This means that my visit has been a genuine success: even the postmaster is in the conspiracy and can't send telegrams. The particular bait to detain me until tomorrow is a cousin, whom I am to see and report on, and see a great deal of: but as soon as I seem to want to see much of anyone I am wanted to see less, so the balance will never adjust itself to my advantage. Ridiculous magical Chhatarpur! Its perfection will make my own

raw *jejune graceless state almost unbearable in com-
parison when I return.*

I did get off that evening. I remember the curious
glow on the pass through the jungle: as though two
halves, light and dark, had been put together to make
each tree. A small animal scuttled over the road. It
came from my lucky direction, so I was all right. At
the same moment a car approached. The animal
came from the car's unlucky direction, so what was
going to happen? The omens seemed to throw up
their hands in despair, the situation became too much
for them and the cars nearly collided.

Next day I was back home—I was beginning to
think of Dewas as home. H.H. was delighted to hear
of my social maneuvering and applauded it. I expected to settle down after this interlude and do a
little work, but almost immediately I dashed off again.

Guest House,
Dhar
October 5th
Wilson *is coming, to our surprise and I may say
consternation. He arrives about the 20th, and we shall
meet him at Bombay, and then I shall settle about*

205

my passage and slip off to Masood's. He is in a very
queer state if one may judge from his letters—practically dotty. I am very sorry for H.H. He is in for
a bad time, merely because he has an exaggerated
estimate of the claims of friendship. It is a sweet
fault and he is one of the sweetest characters upon
this earth. Fearing that I may feel flat, his one thought
is to give me pleasure. I have only just returned from
Chhatarpur, but he has sent me off at once in the
best of his cars to Dhar and wired to its Maharajah,
who is his cousin. I arrived last night.

H.H. (of Dhar) was very polite and called me to
his birthday party, which happened to be in progress.
He was watching a tug of war between the military
and the police. He cares mainly for sport and is also
shy, and I was shy too. Dhar in itself is not interesting
and abominably hot. I came in order to go to Mandu,
and I have been there all today.

Mandu is one of the ruined cities in which India
specialises. It lies on a mountain in the heart of the
Vindhyas, the surrounding wall measures forty miles,
and all within is deserted, and jungle. I had an awful
time entering it. The car got through the mediaeval

gate at the bottom of the ravine, but stuck at a sharp turn higher up, and indeed began to slip back. We rushed for stones, and then for coolies who were repairing another mediaeval gate. There is much too much repairing, but it was well they were there, for they got the car up. I had the Chief Ranger with me as my appointed guide. He was polite and uninteresting as most people seem to be at Dhar. For many hours we puddled about in the car, or walked from building to building.

The architecture is Pathan, date fifteenth century (i.e., contemporary with the dome of the Cathedral of Florence). The scenery and the tremendous forest trees and the great pools of pink lotuses, and the precipices, and the view of the valley of the Nerbudda were wonderful, and a black cobra eight feet long slipped across the road in front of us as a reminder that this is really India. When the evening came, monkeys hooted—it is really between a hoot and a coo—I have never heard it before.

Mandu is 20 miles from Dhar which is 33 from Indore which is 23 from Dewas—76 miles there and the same back. A pretty penny this treat must have cost H.H. and his bankrupt state.

ঙ৵ DASSERA ৡ৵

New Palace,
Dewas
October 10th

Here I am after my wanderings, quite well but exhausted with the hot weather and fidgeted by the general uncertainty of the situation. Tomorrow is the "Dassera," the great National Festivity, and we shall have to put up a coconut in the office and worship it or eat it, I am not sure which. There is a solemn elephant procession up to the shrine on Devi, and a list of the cities and countries subject to Dewas will be read out and sealed by the Finance Member. Our empire extends from Lahore in the north to Poonah in the south and Bengal in the east, but we are moderate compared to the Maharana of Udaipur, who rules (for the purposes of the Dassera) the whole of India. I am frivolous and beg Bapu Sahib to rule all India too, but he says there is no precedent for this. For the last week he has been in Indore, trying to borrow money from the merchants for the purpose of carrying on his administration. I visited him there in his ramshackle house, and he gave me his own bed

—the only one—and slept on the floor. I get to accept such attentions from royalty as a matter of course.

I found Dewas an untidy ant hill, I leave it equally untidy but a desert. All the works have been stopped for lack of funds, and the hideous unfinished palace jags out of the landscape like a mausoleum or a lunatic asylum. It is an appalling tragedy, rooted in the folly of ten years ago. The works should never have been begun. Properly administered, they might have come through, but as it is, they have drained the life of the state. H.H. will certainly reign for the rest of his life in a ruin, and how he is to pay the interest on the loan without overtaxing the cultivator I don't see, and if he overtaxes the cultivator in these days, it means trouble. All this makes the humours of Dassera rather grim. I have too a foreboding that I shall be given a medal and be made to wear a sword. Wilson will of course "cope" with the situation better than I do, but you can't cope much when you have no stones, and what he gains by his efficiency he will lose by his bad temper, for the people here dread him, and all the servants at the Guest House, where he is to live, are trying to leave.

I have been here alone for three days, a little melancholy and waiting for H.H. to turn up from Indore. He did, last night, but has been again away all day at the funeral feast of the late Ruler, which unluckily butts into Dassera, and all the court is with him personating the dead man's ancestors, so the Palace remains pretty quiet. Baldeo is tranquil and very pleasant. Out in the garden, everyone does as little as possible, but what is known as the "October Heat" certainly is trying, and I am in no position to distribute blame. I must, however, see about those coconuts. I find that the motorcars and the electric battery each want to worship one too. Hoping to have caught the spirit of Dassera, I then offered one to the tennis court, and another to the Guest House, but no, wrong again. The tennis court and the Guest House never pray to coconuts, and the garden did its ceremony about a month ago when the horns of my two bullocks were painted green and red for fourpence, a moderate sum.

Since the above, I have been for a solitary row, very soothing, and have watched the birds. They are such spankers—it is a lovely sight. Within five minutes I saw a black and white kingfisher, crossing in its flight a little heron (the "Paddy Bird"), a blue kingfisher sitting upon a submerged mimosa tree, and three enormous cranes; all against an inflamed sky. And when the light failed a quantity of huge fruit bats flew out of a grove and kept dipping in the water. On returning to the shore, I was hailed by a female voice in the English tongue—the European governess of His Highness Junior's boy. She had "often seen me," wanted to speak, etc.: was it not a terribly lonely life, etc., had we a piano? When I said "two," she cried "selfish man." She wanted to be invited for music, but who is to chaperone her? Besides, J.B. would not approve.

I got back to the Palace about 6:30, H.H. shortly after, very piano and tired, poor dear. Between the money-lenders, and Dassera, and the new constitution, and my departure, and the arrival of Malcolm and Josie, Wilson and Luard, he knows not what to think or whither to turn.

Tomorrow sounds awful, though I have got off wearing a sword. The festival is—in its origin—a military review held at the end of the rains, when war under old conditions again became possible, and since everything in India takes a religious tinge, it has turned into a general worship of implements, and of the collective power of the state. I should enjoy it were the state not in debt, but with a heavy load round one's neck it seems so inappropriate. H.H. wants to wear white, in sign of depression, and I am anxious that he should, but fear his brainless relatives will overrule him.

October 13th

We are just through Dassera. I had to act the priest twice. It was enjoyable. The first time I adored a pen, an inkpot, a wastepaper basket and a piece of foolscap, under the direction of my clerk, and administered both to them and him a sacrament of coconut. The coconut kept bouncing up from the office carpet and looking at me when I tried to crack it. Then proceeding to the Electric House I did similar to the switchboard, the dynamo, the batteries, and the engineers. One hasn't to say anything, still less to feel. Just wave incense and sprinkle water and dab with red powder anything you like.

We also drove out a couple of miles against the enemy in landaus, planted a victory tree, and drove back again. In 1907 Malcolm had witnessed a more gorgeous celebration. It began with the ceremonial

ascent of Devi: the nobles and officials worshipped
in the sacred cave on the summit, and five times cir-
cled round a fire of faggots hand in hand: the fifth
time they whetted their swords in the flame. The following day H.H. killed a sheep and Bhau Sahib another, the horses filed past and an attendant held out
a decapitated head and daubed them with blood.
In the afternoon a magnificent procession started,
the band played the state anthem, the army saluted,
H.H., Bhau Sahib, the Chief Priest and the Account-
ant-General rode on an elephant, and all the citi-
zens wore new shoes. When the sun set "the trees
were a dark blur against a sea of gold, the half-moon
serene in an ocean of white cloud." It got dark,
torches smoked and flared, the guns spouted flame
fifteen times, every ten paces as they returned in
triumph through the crowded city they had to stop,
and "a fountain of gold sparks leapt from some magic
pot in front of the elephant." In the Durbar Hall
of the Old Palace homage was paid and gifts con-
ferred: for instance a Mutiny veteran received a silver
dish to be kept in his family for ever. The kiss of
peace was exchanged, and so the wars ended.

Those were the days: and he has also described

the state jewels which he then saw: scarcely any remained in my day. Watched by a committee of six nobles, he inspected trays of necklets, bracelets, nose rings, anklets, all of gold, also rubies and uncut diamonds, and there were ropes and ropes of pearls: for instance ten ropes each four feet long, knotted at the ends with gold: there was a string of watery emeralds as large as marbles: there was a sword studded with diamonds, and a dagger set with rubies: there were the silver trappings for the elephants—three men were needed to lift one: there were gold caparisons for the horses, and trenchers and flagons of gold. Total estimated value: £60,000.

Dassera at Dewas with such wealth behind it, Dassera before the clouds of bankruptcy gathered, may well have succeeded in evoking the martial past. By my day it had shrunk, indeed almost everything was shrinking. Only the religious festival, Gokul Ashtami, which connected the dynasty and its subjects with God, retained its former splendour and was celebrated regardless of cost.

A week later, I was despatched on a mission to Bombay.

Green's Hotel & Restaurant,
Bombay
October 25th

I met the Darlings' boat successfully, going out in a sailing craft on Sunday night with much enterprise, and boarding the City of Birmingham where she lay far out in the middle of the harbour. Nine brides were on board, and as I emerged up the gangway with garlands of flowers upon my arm, I was mistaken by each of them for the bridegroom of the other eight. Josie is sure that the marriages of all will be permanently embittered by the remembrance; each will think, whenever she looks at her husband, "He failed to board the boat when a stray man succeeded."

I have been here since the 21st, desperately busy, wiring, wirelessing, buying motor "accessories," and struggling with incompetence. Being in rather a bad temper, I have not minded: it is when one tries to save people's feelings that life in the East is so exhausting. Colonel Wilson is coming back. Too late to stop him. Not so much incompetence this on H.H.'s part, as a very right desire to consult Malcolm before wiring. Malcolm's boat is a week late, which has dished him. I return to Dewas this afternoon travelling part of the way with the Darlings. I shall clear out of it almost immediately, as I am promised to Masood at Hyderabad and don't want again to disappoint him. Baldeo departed about a week ago and I am to have Hassan until I leave India. He is going to leave in any case on account of Wilson, so I have no scruples. He likes being with me and I like him.

I must stop in a minute and see about carting all my motor tires and spare parts to the station. I hope Wilson will like them, but I have the melancholy suspicion that, whatever I do, he will grumble. He comes back with the intention of quarrelling with all. It is imperative that I should be out of the way. Poor Malcolm and Josie, who have known Wilson in the days when he was a . . .

On this unfinished sentence my last letter from Dewas State Senior ends. My account of the final days there is necessarily sketchy and confused. There was so much that could not then be revealed. I can write freely now and, thanks to detailed notes made at the time, can reconstruct a remarkable sequence. Colonel Wilson has already revealed himself as a problem. He was actually much more than that. He hung over us like a nightmare, like a gathering storm cloud, which finally burst grotesquely.

✑ COLONEL WILSON ✒

To explain, I must go back many years.

Malcolm and he first met in 1910 up in the mountains, beyond Simla, over a boundary dispute. Wilson called one morning about breakfast time, but Malcolm did not offer him any, because he had none: his arrangements had gone wrong and he was himself starving. In a day or two he received an icy letter, pillorying him for his lack of hospitality. He replied, stating the facts. The Colonel rode over again, almost in tears, and they became warm friends. Indeed, Wilson must have had much charm and many noble qualities. He would give away all he had, he was selfless and fearless, he had hunted big game on foot, he had tamed every animal in India save the crocodile, children adored him, he was a brilliant raconteur, and a vigorous penman.

At Malcolm's suggestion, he went to Dewas in the autumn of 1920. His official career was at an end, but his private life had been tragic and he had little to call him to England, and though to be Private

Secretary to a native state was beneath his dignity, and though he held the usual view of Indians, he settled down happily with the Maharajah and soon became devoted to him. They were Father William and White Prince to one another and Wilson even thought of building in Dewas City a memorial drinking trough. He planned the immense garden round the New Palace, he reorganised the Guest House, the motorcars, the municipality, he supervised the education of Vikky and selected a governess to do the actual teaching. He sped up and down India to further the state's welfare, and during one of the journeys he got out of a restaurant car while it was in motion and was crushed between the platform and the train. Believed to be dying, he was carried into a waiting room and pencilled the words: "My last thought is for you, White Prince." The Maharajah hastened from Dewas to nurse him. He recovered, but it was not thought prudent that he should risk hot weather. He went off to England in February and was to return in the autumn, and he was invested before his departure with the highest honour but one that the state could confer: the Tukojirao III Gold Medal.

When I came out a month later as a stopgap, I

found the court full of the Colonel's praises. He was loyal, able, helpful, also sympathetic, witty and full of fun. He and Malarao were always at play and it was suggested that Malarao and I should play with each other too, which we did a little, out of politeness. As for his practical activities there was no doubt: the ground was littered with them for acres. I asked for a plan, a memorandum, particularly of his intentions regarding the garden. None was forthcoming, but almost at once letters began to arrive from him, enquiring how his "beloved garden" was getting on. I waited until I had got a clearer view of the chaos, and then wrote him the longest letter I have ever written in my life, pages and pages of detail, interspersed with numerous enquiries. I also got him his money. About 1,500 rupees were owing to him. He thought, and H.H. thought, that it had been placed to his account in Bombay, but when he tried to draw a cheque it was dishonoured, which, as he remarked, is not a pleasant experience after thirty years in the country.

Shortly afterwards, all the works, including his own, were closed down. As far as the garden was concerned, it did not matter, for there was an inexplicable slip in the Colonel's schemes which made closure auto-matic: he had forgotten the water supply. There were, as my letters have told, rows of taps and masses of pipes, and they connected with a raised cistern, a noble object on four legs, but there the sequence ended: the cistern was empty, nor could it be filled. We did our watering from two small wells which dried up in May. I put this to him as tactfully as I could. He replied thanking me for my charming let-ter and promising to read *Howards End* as soon as possible. He said he was much disappointed that the works were not getting on, and the reason was in-trigue. Much of his letter was in French. We con-tinued to correspond with civility, but on my side with less freedom: he seemed so easily upset. To the Maharajah he wrote: "So all my plans are set aside. In all the years that I served Queen Victoria (of sainted memory) I have never experienced one frac-tion of the mortification and humiliation that I un-derwent while serving you, my dear White Prince. Your heartbroken Father William." And again, "When H.R.H. the Prince of Wales comes to India, does he propose to visit Dewas? If he does, I shall cut my throat. To see the palace and grounds that you planned as a monument of piety become a dunghill and a rubbish heap and a laughingstock of those vile sneering Politicals from Indore, is more than my soul can bear, as your saintly mother and mine, both together with God, well know."

I began to pity him—he was obviously overwrought and unwell, but his idealism made me uneasy. Whom would he attack next? Sometimes he spoke of England—still so glorious despite the canker at her core —or had a "most important plan" to communicate, which the Maharajah must keep secret even from his trusted Malarao and Morgan Forster—some plan of anti-national propaganda which the Houses of Windsor and Dewas were to work together, and which had been highly approved by a general to whom he had shown it. At other times gloom prevailed: he had quarrelled with Malcolm (then in England), he was in pain, and did his White Prince want him back really? Whenever this question was asked, H.H. would pull himself together and send a cable containing such sentences as, "I love you more than ever and long to have you with me," and costing several pounds. Malcolm also wrote, confirming our impression of ill health, and hinting that the Colonel seemed rather distressed because I had dismissed the motor driver Kanaya whom he had particularly chosen with an eye to the Maharajah's safety.

H.H. once said of himself, "I am always hypnotising myself into the belief that a situation is bearable," and I think this analysis is sound. At any rate I can trace four stages in the reputation of Wilson at Dewas. (1) He liked and was liked by all. (2) He had many enemies but H.H. liked him. (3) H.H. didn't really like him but recognised his high qualities. (4) He hadn't even high qualities. Local murmurs arose. The Political Agent said, "He's far too old to come back." The manager of the Electric Company hinted at an awful scene in their Bombay office, which if it had not been for the Colonel's infirmity would have ended in blows. The Maharajah, out of sheer mischievousness, accused him of being au mieux with a lady. "But how did you know this?" H.H.: "I opened his letters one day for a joke, and there was one from her beginning 'My own darling.' Then I apologised."—"But that was bad of you."—"Yes, Morgan, I know it was bad of me and I said so. I repented, still I did it and that's how I know."

In Dewas it turned out that he had quarrelled with nearly everyone, and though he had been efficient owing to his knowledge of the language and to previous experience as a cantonment magistrate, he had kept H.H. so busy as a peacemaker that he made more work than he did. His bitterest quarrel was with Deolekr Sahib, his personal assistant. It began with a ride upon an elephant where there had been some misunderstanding with the mahout. Colonel Wilson wanted to go back, the elephant continued to advance, and he thought that Deolekr (he was humorous and young) was contriving this to tease him, and nearly fell from the howdah in his rage.

He began to write letters that were full of a touching jealousy: "I am sure you prefer Morgan Forster." He campaigned against me as a weak literary man, who had been seduced by Deolekr to join the other side, who was too idle to plant mangoes and lemons in the garden, and too frivolous to retain good chauffeurs. Whatever H.H. thought of me himself, he would not stand my being criticised, since it reflected on his own judgment, and I think too he was fond of me, though one can never be certain of saints. "The poor old Colonel must come back," he said, "but he only wants to stop for the cold weather, and that is best. He returns in the spirit of revenge, and I shall have an awful time, an awful time, for I will no longer protect him against my own people. As for you—I thought you would meet him, and hand over, but that is now impossible. I cannot have you insulted. And yet to let you leave my state before he comes is a disgrace to me. He will notice a great change in my manner."

The Colonel never grasped that I did not want Dewas as a permanency. I was well content that he should return and I continued to uphold his memory and to write him friendly notes. When Malarao and I played about, which we now did because we liked it, catching at one another's bare feet, knocking off one another's turbans, and rolling on the drawing-room carpet in the centre of a circle of seventeen cross-legged and hilarious nobles, I never allowed Malarao to say that Father William would not have gone so far with an Indian. My conscience was clear. And all seemed well. On August the 4th he wrote me a most friendly letter which began "Dear Forster" and ended "Hoping you are fit and with many thanks for what you have done for me."

But a month later he wrote to me as follows.

London
September 6th, 1921

Dear Mr. Forster,

In thanking you for your note received about a week ago, I am sorry I have no time to reply except on a very important subject.

You enclosed the contents of a cover addressed to me by name, and with no mention even of my official job.

I know that some people feel when they get east of Suez that not only the ten commandments are obsolete but also the obligations and etiquette of English society. You had twice before opened my private letters, but on the second occasion—a letter addressed most obviously by an English lady—you felt some qualms as to your action and I refrained from remark. These qualms now seem to have subsided. I can only think that the hypnotic power of your surroundings has affected you, but as I may now have a number of

*most private letters awaiting my arrival, may I ask you
most kindly to refrain from opening them, and if you
think H.H. wishes you to act otherwise kindly obtain
written authority in each case.*

Yours sincerely,

W. WILSON

When this thunderbolt fell, H.H. was at his two
hours' prayer, and could not be approached. ("I am
so very sorry I am holy just now," he would say if one
did approach him.) As soon as we met he exclaimed,
"I've had a letter from Wilson. He, Malcolm and
Josie are now all coming out on the same boat. He
says that he shall undertake no more administrative
work since it is not appreciated, but shall continue
to supervise the Prince's education. It is an unpleasant
letter."

"So is this," I said, and handed him mine. He read
it in a flash and went grey. The reference to the "hypnotic power of my surroundings" gave him the most
direct annoyance, but his deepest feeling was a generous indignation for my sake. I looked upset. I must
be distracted and comforted. He did not worry me
with questions; whether I had pried into the Colonel's

correspondence deliberately, for instance: this did not interest him in the least. No, he telegraphed to his cousin of Dhar, and while I was still in a daze arranged that I should go over there as a state guest. I visited Dhar, as already mentioned, and Mandu, and toiled for hours over its rocks and stupendous scenery. Mandu occupies the whole breadth of the Vindhyas. On the north a chasm divides it from the Central Indian tableland: on the south a precipice drops straight into the valley of the Nerbudda, beyond which the Maratha homelands begin. I registered nothing, not even when the black cobra nearly ran over my feet. All the time I was composing and rejecting replies to Colonel Wilson. At first I favoured something elaborately satiric. Mixed with my memories of the Delhi Gate is something about "if he was lucky, he would find when he reached Dewas that I had appropriated the office cash." I did not send this sentence. I tried to remind myself that he was old and ill, but the oftener I read his note the better I found his English. Should I reply genially, saying that his excellent style was alone unforgiveable? I rejected this while peering into a chasm where the

Maharani of Dhar had shot a tiger last week. There
is no doubt that he had succeeded in hurting me.
I do not forgive people for doing that, nor have I
even now forgiven him for spoiling Mandu. The evening cries of its monkeys, its marvellous long-term
echo, are dulled by this middle-class row.

On regaining Dewas I composed a stinker. H.H.
supervised it, and decried any attempt at moderation:
"No, no, he will never understand, he will regard it
as your weakness." We despatched my effort in du-
plicate to London and to Bombay, since we thought
he might now be on the high seas.

Dewas Senior
October 7th, 1921

Dear Colonel Wilson

I have received your letter of September 6th and
will hand to H.H. any of your correspondence that
may precede you at Dewas. Your bicycle and lamp,
hitherto in my room, will be given to Malarao Sahib.

As regards your private letters, opened by me, I
herewith make the following statement. I opened
them in the belief that they were of an official nature,
bearing on my work. Finding that they were not, I

did not read them. I have no knowledge as to their contents, nor, until you informed me, was I aware of the sex of your correspondents.

If you believe the above statement, I demand from you a full and unqualified apology for your letter of September 6th, as regards both its matter and its manner. If you do not believe it, I neither expect nor desire to hear from you again.

A copy of this correspondence will be forwarded to Mr. Darling. It is on his acount that I provide you with this opportunity for apologising.

Yours sincerely,

E. M. FORSTER

Soon after my letter was posted, we learnt that the Colonel was after all not coming out on the Darlings' boat, but on a later boat, and the next piece of news was that he was engaged to be married. This last, confided as an intimate and sacred secret, was promptly announced by the infuriated White Prince to the assembled court. "Am I to support his wife too?" he cried. He now resolved to set out in person for Bombay, meet the Darlings' boat, explain the imbroglio, and get Malcolm's permission to cancel the

Colonel's return: there would be just time for a cable before the later boat sailed.

But he had reckoned without his religious observances. The anniversary of his mother's death corresponded with the date of Malcolm's arrival. It was impossible for him to leave Dewas and that was why I had to go to Bombay alone. Oh, what a complicated expedition! At midnight I slipped off from the Apollo Quay in the sailing boat. I was not only carrying the garlands of jasmine, roses and tinsel; in my pocket was Colonel Wilson's letter to me and a copy of my reply to it. I administered the garlands first, and when everyone was wearing them, the letters. Malcolm pulled a very stiff lip. "A lamentable correspondence," he said. He must have been vexed with me for my indiscretion at opening envelopes addressed to someone else, but he did not say so, only that he was amazed the Colonel had done it. For the Colonel had, half-laughingly, imparted his suspicions about me to him in London ("I suppose your Morgan Forster's all square"), and Malcolm had assured him of my squareness, and thought all was well.

Then came the most difficult part of my mission.

I had to break it that H.H. no longer wanted Wilson back, and that he was only awaiting Malcolm's permission to cable to him and dismiss him. Malcolm grew warm at this, said that there wasn't time, and that the shock and the insult might well kill the Colonel, who was an old man and had been ill—ill health contracted in the Maharajah's service—and who was also deeply in love and hoping for a happy close to his life. I emphasised that I wanted Wilson to come. My temporary job was over, I shouldn't be meeting him, and after Hyderabad I should be leaving India for good. But I felt awkward.

Telegrams now flew between the S.S. *City of Birmingham* and the Palace of Dewas. Malcolm had to proceed at once to his duties in the Punjab. The commemorative mourning was now over, so the Maharajah was free to leave Dewas, but where should they meet? The Punjab mail stopped at Rutlam, and it was arranged that H.H. should board it there, and should travel as far as the next stopping-place, to discuss Wilson's return. My last memory of the affair, and of Dewas generally, takes the form of a scrambling senseless railway journey. H.H. turned up at

Rutlam "almost alone": that is to say only Malarao, Deolekr, Nadka, Babaji Rao, Ambunana the Priest, Boy the Goanese, and some other servants attended him. He had taken tickets for us on the mail and we were to return to Rutlam by the down-mail.

I expected him to yield as soon as he heard Malcolm's opinion, but he revealed himself as every inch a king, grew vehement, and said that never since the Maharani had left had he been so upset, and that he absolutely would not have the Colonel back.

"Answer this one question, Malcolm. If I put him off now, shall I be behaving in an ungentlemanly fashion?"

Malcolm considered carefully before replying, "I know nothing you do could be ungentlemanly, but it will certainly be considered so by other English people who hear of it."

"No matter," said H.H. "Their opinion is not of the least importance. I cable at the next stopping-place."

By now we had advanced in a northeasterly direction far into the interior of India, and paid again and again supplementary fares. The Dewas party and

myself got out at a desolate station, the Punjab
party went on in a condition of chill, and I began to
draft the cable in a little telegraph office, while my
various friends looked over my shoulder and made
suggestions. The cable began: "Owing to temporary
financial difficulties in my state am reluctantly com-
pelled to forgo pleasure of having European officer,"
and cost £25. It had to be expressed (treble rate),
and also duplicated to London and to Trieste, since
the Colonel might already have started. It contained
a compensation offer of £100, which Malcolm had
emphasised was the very least we could send: steam-
ship fare had already been paid. At last I got it off,
and we returned to our capital in a deflated condition. H.H. was very low. "It is all my own fault, all
my own weakness," he said, and it partly was, for
throughout the summer Wilson had kept enquiring
whether he had better return. It was also Wilson's
fault, for being jealous, suspicious, and disagreeable.
It was also my fault, for opening letters too casually,
and for not apologising for my errors of judgment
with sufficient formality and profuseness. None of us
had any reason to be proud. And Malcolm—upon

whom the unpleasantness really fell—can have had no reason to feel proud of his three friends.

So my time at Dewas ended, but damply. Affection and respect survived, and I was duly invested before my departure with the highest honour but one that the state could confer, the Tukojirao III Gold Medal. I still treasure it. It is a temporary medal—the sun's face is scratched on it by a pin. Nor has it any proper ribbon, only a crumpled wisp of red. I was promised that in time the real medal would be struck, and that then I should exchange. I shall never exchange. The highest honour of all was the Tukojirao III Gold Medal inset with a diamond: the Dewan had been awarded that, and I can think of no one who could have better deserved it. Honourable, dignified, diligent, prudent, austere, he had served the state unceasingly.

Colonel Wilson did not answer my letter. But I know that his health improved, and that he settled down for the rest of his life in England, respected and liked by those who understood him.

The last letter of mine that I shall print is from Hyderabad. Alas! It registers relief.

Hyderabad,

Deccan

November 12th

I am having a lovely time here and enjoying every moment of it. Masood in such good form, the weather perfect and exhilarating, beautiful things to look at, interesting people to talk to, delicious food, romantic walks, pretty birds in the garden, no Baldeo and no religion. Not but what Mr. Hydari,* when least expected to do so, unlaces his boots and prostrates himself in a tight tweed suit during a picnic, but when it is over it is over, and he does not require red powder or drums to see him through. I have passed abruptly from Hinduism to Islam and the change is a relief. I have come too into a world whose troubles and problems are intelligible to me: Dewas made much ado about nothing and no ado where a little would have been seemly.

My last letters told you nothing of my departure. We were both very melancholy. I hated leaving him, but it is his tragedy not to know how to employ peo-

---

* Afterwards (the first) Sir Akbar Hydari; he and Lady Hydari were the kindest of friends to me and to my mother: I stayed with their son, the second Sir Akbar, on my last visit to India, in 1945.

235

ple, and I could not feel it any use to go on muddling with work that gave me no satisfaction, and was of no essential importance to him. The things of this life mean so little to him—mean something so different, anyway—I never feel certain what he likes, or even whether he likes me; consideration for others so often simulates affection in him. I only know that he is one of the sweetest and saintliest men I have ever known, and that his goodness is not mawkish, but goes with deep insight into character and knowledge of the world. It is very difficult to describe him because he does belong to another civilisation in a way that other Indians I have met do not.

About the Prince of Wales' visit I might also write much. It is disliked and dreaded by nearly everyone. The chief exceptions are the motor firms and caterers, who will make fortunes, and the non-cooperators and extremists, who will have an opportunity for protest which they would otherwise have lacked. Masood is an exception too, because he believes that the Prince will make some important announcement, perhaps in regard to Turkey: if he doesn't do something dramatic and fundamental, his visit will be worse than useless, Masood agrees. The National Congress meets in December at Ahmedabad, and it will certainly carry through its resolution in favour of Civil Disobedience, and if there is general response, this expensive royal expedition will look rather foolish.

I have been with pro-Government and pro-English Indians all this time, so cannot realise the feeling of the other party: and am only sure of this—that we were paying for the insolence of Englishmen and Englishwomen out here in the past. I don't mean that good manners can avert a political upheaval. But they can minimise it, and come nearer to averting it in the East than elsewhere. English manners out here have improved wonderfully in the last eight years. Some people are frightened, others seem really to have undergone a change of heart.

But it's too late. Indians don't long for social intercourse with Englishmen any longer. They have made a life of their own.

NOTE ON A PASSAGE TO INDIA

I began this novel before my 1921 visit, and took out the opening chapters with me, with the intention of continuing them. But as soon as they were confronted with the country they purported to describe, they seemed to wilt and go dead and I could do nothing with them. I used to look at them of an evening in my room at Dewas, and felt only distaste and despair. The gap between India remembered and India experienced was too wide. When I got back to England the gap narrowed, and I was able to resume. But I still thought the book bad, and probably should not have completed it without the encouragement of Leonard Woolf.

I dedicated it to Masood. In one of the later editions (the "Everyman") I added the Maharajah's name to his. By that time both of them had died.

CATASTROPHE

When I returned to England the first news I had
about Dewas concerned its new constituion. Not a
success. Lord Reading had after all not come and the
table decorations had been ill-advised. In an attempt
to be original someone had thought out a scheme of
live ducklings in glass troughs. They were to swim up
and down during the inaugural banquet and entertain
the guests with their drolleries. But the water was too
cold, the ducklings huddled in a bunch and the guests
had to pick them out and warm them in their servi-
ettes. One of them nearly died. It reminded me of
my own failure with the ornamental fish at Gokul
Ashtami.

As for the constitution, it was one of a batch which
was improvised to greet the Prince of Wales. Gwalior,
Bhopal, most of the adjacent states produced one.
It was tripartite and consisted of the Ruler, a State
Council of six, and a Representative Assembly of
about seventy. The Ruler was supreme. The Council
consisted of a member nominated by him, a member

of the Ruling House, a noble, a nominated official, and two town and village members nominated by the Assembly. The Council could legislate, but he had a veto, and it could not alter his annual grant except to increase it. As for the Representative Assembly, it consisted of an official to represent the Ruler, a member of the Ruling House, twenty nobles, twenty-one officials, eight members elected by the towns, and twenty elected by the villages. It had no executive or legislative powers. As a further safeguard against democracy, all members both of the Council and of the Assembly were to be nominated, not elected, for the next five years, since the people were not yet sufficiently educated to vote. Thus did Dewas prepare itself to meet the modern world.

Nevertheless cheerful reports continued to arrive from the Darlings. Though stationed in the Punjab, they kept in touch. Bapu Sahib was evidently in splendid form. He had much fun and gained some prestige over a crisis in the affairs of the Maharajah of Indore. Indore got into serious trouble with the Government of India, and called him in to mediate. He dashed around detecting or initiating intrigues, and greatly enjoyed himself. Another time he got some amusement out of *A Passage to India*. He dined at the Viceregal Lodge at Delhi soon after it had been published, and found that it was ill thought of there. Lady Reading did not care for it at all, and the newly appointed Indian Member of Council expressed himself severely. He let them discourse as they would and then sweetly said that the author had been his Private Secretary. "That comes of Chiefs getting the wrong kind of Europeans around them," Lord Reading interjected. And H.H. rejoined, "But it is then Your Excellency's fault, for we cannot employ any European without your concurrence." And he proceeded to praise the work warmly.

In Dewas itself things seemed normal. There was for instance the periodical scare over His Highness Junior. A shy unobtrusive monarch, seldom seen, seldom mentioned, and probably quite devoid of ambition or guile, J.B. would occasionally make some slight gesture which convulsed the nervous Senior Branch. This time—it was Christmas—he sent a courtier with a letter to their Private Secretary begging for the names of their guests in order that he might have the pleasure of giving each of them a Christmas

card. It seemed an innocent project, but Bapu Sahib
knew better. "Ah! sister, this is serious," he confided
to Josie Darling. "J.B. wants to know something. This
is some dangerous intrigue. Yesterday he wrote to me
himself, but I knew he was up to something and did
not reply." For some hours he was plunged in gloom,
then he cheered up and even joined in a laugh against
himself.

What was dangerous at Dewas? What was harm-
less? The future was soon to reveal.

❧ THE YUVRAJ ☙

Vikky, henceforward to be referred to as the Yuvraj
(Crown Prince), had now developed from a shy child
into a charming well-mannered and intelligent youth.
He made an excellent impression on everyone. For
a time he lived in the Guest House with three of his
half sisters: he and Bai Saheba's family had always
been good friends. When he reached the age of sixteen an alliance was sought for him, and he was duly
affianced to the daughter of the Chief of Jath, a
Maratha landowner in the Deccan. The girl was well
educated and charming, her parents were excellent
people, all seemed prosperous, and the marriage was

celebrated at Dewas at the end of 1926 in the presence of a vast concourse of notables.

I don't know how many rajahs are here [writes Mal-
colm]. *Patiala and Kapurthala luckily declined. Ranis
are nothing accounted of, and Europeans, happily
not yet arrived, are legion. This morning Tukoji entered unexpectedly, clad entirely in white except for
a green turban, but with darkened brow: the Gwalior
party, instead of eight guests and twenty servants, was
to be thirteen guests and fifty-five servants, and could
they all have tea at 6:30 tomorrow morning. To make
matters worse the P.A., who had written that he and
his wife were too ill to come, wired to say that they
had now recovered and proposed attending.*

The ceremonies took place without any of the
presages that had haunted the Maharajah's own nup-
tials at Kolhapur. No one—that is to say, no decent
person—could have foreseen what was coming.

It was really interesting and beautiful too [Josie writes
to her son] *but O! what an awful time Vikky has had
for about a week, bathing and praying and sitting like
a graven image with strings of pearls hanging over*

his face and his forehead painted red and gold. Last
night I saw him and his bride process round the fire,
and have their garments knotted together and take
their final vows. This I saw inside the purdah. Then
came the procession—very jolly. Vikky and bride on
an elephant, his sisters and their bridegrooms on two
more, lots of other brides and grooms in carriages,
then the army, bands, more elephants, more bands.
In front of Vikky's elephant two enormous ticklers
of tinsel, thirty feet high, were carried, and round his
howdah clung a swarm of chuprassis waving peacock
feather switches. We walked in the procession as re-
lations for a bit: had a fearfully narrow squeak of
being then put into the purdah bus. All those ceremonies are a pleasant mixture of ritual and informal-
ity: for instance at one stage the entire procession
halted to allow Uncle Tukky and me to light ciga-
rettes.

The contracting parties agreed that the consum-
mation of the marriage should be postponed for two
years: the Yuvraj would then have come of age and
be independent of his father's control, and he should
also have taken his B.A. degree. The Chief of Jath

wanted the bride to stay with her parents during the
interval, but after she had been with them a short
time the Maharajah became anxious about the prestige of his state, and insisted that she should return
to Dewas although there was no suitable establish-
ment there for her. She was put into the Guest
House, none of her family attended her, and her husband was only allowed to see her when other people
were present. The situation soon degenerated into a
wretched muddle, this or that was tried, nothing
worked, nerves got on edge, tempers were frayed,
the Yuvraj could not concentrate on his studies. The
bride then made a dramatic and unexpected gesture:
on her return from a pilgrimage she laid an open
letter on the dynastic altar at the Old Palace, in which
she swore eternal fidelity to her husband and called
down the vengeance of Shri Krishna upon any member of either family who should try to separate them.
The letter distressed the Maharajah: although his
conscience was clear, he felt it might be a reflection
on himself and his manner became grave. After various half measures and changes of mood and displays
of weakness, he adopted the only sensible course and

allowed his daughter-in-law to go back to her parents at Jath.

But it was too late. Shortly after her departure—on December the 21st, 1927, to be precise—the catastrophe came. The Yuvraj fled. Fled from Dewas, declaring that he was being poisoned by his father. Fled to Indore and sought the protection of the Government of India and of its representative, the A.G.G.

The situation was appalling, and so confused that it is impossible, even at this distance of time, to get it clear. Three points stand out. Firstly, the young man was genuinely frightened. Secondly, he had no cause whatsoever for fear. Thirdly, his mind had been warped by emissaries from Kolhapur. Those emissaries were always hanging about: I can never remember a time when there wasn't one. For the most part they watched and reported. Sometimes they went further and insinuated. On this occasion—for the second time in their infamous existence perhaps—they struck and killed.

The Maharajah collapsed. As soon as he recovered he wired for Malcolm and Josie, and they started at once from Lahore. Meanwhile the A.G.G. at Indore,

Mr. Reginald Glancy,* was confronted with the situation on his return from some college sports. He handled it with presence of mind, with wisdom and with sympathy. He received the agitated Yuvraj into the Residency, calmed his preposterous fears, prevented him from heading for Kolhapur, and arranged a meeting between him and his father. This was a failure: the young man's suspicions were renewed, and he collapsed in his turn. Father and son were, however, agreed on one point: there could be no return to Dewas after this hideous misunderstanding, and Mr. Glancy welcomed the Maharajah's suggestion that the Government of India should undertake guardianship. "Naturally," writes the Maharajah, "I never wished anything but well to the boy, and under these circumstances I want the Paramount Government to take my place and direct his education and training, reasonable expenses for the same and his maintenance being given." The suggestion was sensible and dignified, and it seemed that a scandal would be avoided, but unfortunately, and character-

---

* Afterwards Sir Reginald Glancy. His brother, Sir Bertrand Glancy, was connected with Dewas affairs at a later date, and adopted a very different attitude towards them.

istically, H.H. began making stipulations. The Yuvraj
was not to go to Kolhapur where his mother was, nor
to Jath where his wife was; he was to be regarded as
a political offender: his accomplices were to be ex-
tradicted and punished, and there was to be no enquiry. This last stipulation must have disconcerted
Mr. Glancy. Why no enquiry? Had the Maharajah
after all something to conceal? It was a disastrous
move—innocence masquerading as guilt. Naturally
the Government of India could not be bound; it
would undertake the guardianship unconditionally or
not at all. Negotiations broke down, the Yuvraj proceeded to Kolhapur, and the *Times of India* carried
such headings as "Unpleasant Happenings in Indian
States—A Dewas Scandal."

So when Malcolm and Josie arrived from Lahore,
they found everything had been mismanaged; all the
cards played wrong, their friend almost out of his
mind, declaring that he would abdicate, that he would
appeal to the Princes of India to prevent an enquiry, that Mr. Glancy was his sworn enemy. They
reasoned with him, and then they waxed wroth:
"The distressing thing was, we had to say such
wounding things to him," Josie writes, "such as

that he had always neglected Vikky and that he accepted mere rumours as gospel truth, but he took it with his usual angelic sweetness. He is I think one of the most loveable, most original and most unwise men I have ever met." He poured out his account of the catastrophe. After the bride's final departure to Jath, the bridegroom remained at the Guest House, increasingly discontented, and increasingly under the influence of a Kolhapur agent. A "loyal Sirdar" was appointed to counteract the agent —a typical device, and a fatuous one: why not have sacked the agent? The Yuvraj then felt unwell and was easily persuaded that his father was poisoning him; he leapt in terror into a car and dashed for the frontier, and as they crossed the Sipra, the fatal Sipra, the agent fired a pistol into the mudguard so that it might appear that an ambush had been laid for them down in the ravine. Punctured with bullet holes, they reached the Residency at Indore, and the rest we know.

Such was the Maharajah's story. It may be inaccurate, and the bullet-riddled mudguard does not appear elsewhere. The misery, the innocence, the shame—they are authentic: shame for his state, which a dastardly intrigue had laid low. Malcolm did what he could, and he and Charles Goodall (of Bombay) had some correspondence with the editor of the *Times of India*, and pointed out some of the more obvious libels and inaccuracies contained in its report. Unfortunately Malcolm, as a civil servant, could not write publicly, and the editor, though sympathetic, declined to publish an unsigned correction.

The Government of India behaved decently. Writing to the Maharajah on April 9th, 1928, Mr. Reginald Glancy notes with approval that "an allowance of two thousand five hundred rupees per mensem has been fixed for the maintenance of husband and wife," and he adds, "It is not intended by Government to take any notice of the absurd reports which have appeared in the press, and Government have already taken all steps in their power to discourage any continuation of the press campaign." But the mud stuck. Kolhapur interests were strong in racing and other circles at Bombay, the "absurd reports" spread, until it was assumed at dinner parties and in clubs that the Maharajah of Dewas Senior was an infamous villain. On one occasion April * (Malcolm

* Now Madame van Biervliet.

252

and Josie's daughter) was sitting by a distinguished and responsible official who complacently expressed this view. Inwardly she raged, and at the age of eighteen deflated him in a way which he was unlikely to forget.

Before leaving the subject of the Yuvraj, I have something most pleasant and cheering to add. He became Maharajah (as Vikramsinharao) when his father died, ruled well, and went to North Africa in the Second World War, and fought there with courage and distinction. When I revisited India in 1945, I kept away from Dewas, for I could not suppose that I should now be welcome there. He heard of this, and sent a courteous message that he should have been glad to see me, as his father's friend. Two years later he came to London for the victory celebrations, with Deolekr Sahib as his A.D.C. Strange Indian aftermath! We met at a sports club near Ealing, and then I had lunch with them in Park Lane. I had not seen him since 1913. Now he had grown into a splendid and generous-minded prince, so like his father physically that I kept forgetting that a generation had passed and that I was addressing a stranger. He was warm and friendly, he was healthy and active—

much more the happy warrior type—and he had determined to put an end to the old quarrels and to wipe out family bitterness and bickering. With this in view, he invited me to go out to Dewas and to stay there as his guest and to write his father's life: whom he rightly considered to be a great man. On this happy note my memories of him close. Soon after his London visit he became Maharajah of Kolhapur, his mother's state, Kolhapur, fountain of honours and of troubles. He was succeeded at Dewas by his son. With the transference of power both states have lost their identity and have been merged in modern India and their feud is no more. May all that was good in them—and there was much good—combine to fertilise the future!

⊷ৡ PONDICHERRY ৡ⊷

The Maharajah's prestige never recovered from this domestic scandal. The final blow to his fortunes, however, was economic. His financial position had been bad even in my day, it had got worse, he had spent immense sums on the Yuvraj's marriage and on the birth of a son to Bai Saheba and on secret-service agents at Delhi and elsewhere. And then came the slump of agricultural prices. It came in 1930, and lasted four years. All the agrarian areas suffered. Dewas, being already insecure, went bankrupt. In one year the land revenue of the state was halved and its total income fell from about ten lakhs to six,* officials were not paid, cultivators were overtaxed, land alienated. By 1933 the position was so grave that the Government of India was obliged to intervene.

Two courses were open to it. It might have approached the Maharajah informally and on friendly terms, and thus established personal contact. He wanted help, he knew he was in a mess, largely through his own fault, but he was too proud to ask help from those who would respond not as friends but as officials, and he was in arms at once if help was forced on him: "I do not mind for myself but my state is being insulted," he would cry. And he would point out indignantly that other rulers—Alwar for instance—had behaved far worse but had got off scot-free because they were powerful, and that he himself—unlike others—had never wavered in his loyalty to the Crown. Unfortunately most of the A.G.G.s and P.A.s he had had to deal with were not the sort of

* A lakh = £7,500.

people whom he wanted as friends or negotiators; nor can I feel surprised; I have experienced them myself. They were insensitive, or if they were sensitive, they were clever-clever and tried to beat him at his own tricks, and one or two of them were cads. There were exceptions—there was Major Luard, who could have done anything with him, and there was Mr. Reginald Glancy, whose good offices he had rejected—but on the whole they constituted an unattractive body of men.

So the Government rejected the friendly personal approach and took the alternative course, and issued orders which became widely known and which dishonoured him in the eyes of his subjects and his fellow Chiefs: he was to apply for an Accounts Officer who would examine the financial situation and prepare a report; or alternatively, he was to apply for a Dewan and undertake not to dismiss him: in a communication of July 24th he is ordered to decide within a fortnight. He did not decide, and although the period of grace was extended to a month he still did not decide, for his back was up. He wrote courteously and prevaricated in the hope of getting a loan of two or three lakhs. The Government then grew sterner, and ordered him to accept a commission of enquiry "under Government of India Resolution No. 426.R of 1921." A copy of No. 426.R was enclosed "in case Your Highness has not a copy." But before it could be read by him he had taken a fatal and a fantastic step.

The temple of Ramesvaram is one of the holiest places in India. Rama founded it when he was on his way to search for Sita in Ceylon. It stands on an island at the extreme south of the peninsula—a wonderful Saivite shrine with three courtyards and immense colonnades and majestic gateways and a lingam washed daily with Ganges water. In the September of 1933, the Maharajah decided to make a pilgrimage to Ramesvaram. Off he went: Bai Saheba and her growing family accompanied him, also his brother and various courtiers. The decision was unwise, but worse was to follow: he never got there. After a couple of days' travelling he complained of ill health, and turned aside to Pondicherry, the capital of French India, for medical treatment. No doubt he was unwell—the reports of the Pondicherry doctor are explicit, and he had certainly had enough worry to cause a breakdown. But other motives operated: impishness; a desire to elude the Government and to negotiate with it from safety; perhaps even a wild hope that from this corner of France he might overthrow it and bring it and all its A.G.G.s and P.A.s tumbling to the ground. Anyhow, there he was—a thousand miles away from his beloved kingdom and in a part of India unknown to him, and there he dug himself in and died. The place had few attractions for a king in exile. A distinguished saint and man of letters, Aurobindo Ghose, lived there, but they did not become intimate. He remained shut up with his family and his dwindling train of attendants, immersed in his religious observances and his political intrigues.

The Government was furious and commanded his return. He was to be back in Dewas by November 10th. He refused, and ordered his State Council to dissolve itself if there was any external interference. He also despatched an immense telegram to the Viceroy, Lord Willingdon: his swan song in telegrams. "I at the very outset beg your Excellency to forgive this rather lengthy wire," it begins, recapitulates the dispute, refuses to make any concession, asks for a loan, refuses to leave Pondicherry, and concludes, after one thousand words, with "Situated as you are in the highest position of trust for the British prestige and honour and for the welfare, dignity and rights of the Indian Rulers, I have no other course left open and beg to be excused for the same." Lord Willingdon's secretary replied that His Excellency saw no reason to modify the decision already made. The wheels of Western righteousness rolled on and crushed him.

His friends were appalled at the trap which he had contrived for himself. The situation had been dangerous enough while he remained at home: in Pondicherry it had become disastrous. Dewas was lost: a provisional government had been installed there under the Yuvraj. We wrote and wired urging him to compromise, to give in to the inevitable, and so save something out of the wreck. My letters came back to me after his death: they make odd reading now. He ignored our advice, and naturally, for royal blood boiled in his veins and not in ours. He was descended from the sun. Malcolm interceded on his behalf with various officials, high and low, and pointed out to them the importance, in such a case as this, of kindness and sympathy. There had been

plenty of rectitude over the Dewas Senior bankruptcy, but no imagination and scant courtesy: on one
occasion a high official who was dealing with the case
actually drove through Dewas without calling. They
listened—preferably down a telephone—but they knew
that they had behaved correctly, so had nothing to
say. They were impeccably right and absolutely
wrong. I do not suggest that he would have fared
better under a purely Indian government: the late
Mr. Vallabhai Patel would have given him even
shorter shrift. But the British, who were then in
power, did destroy him.

A year later Malcolm, at some personal inconven-
ience, went to Pondicherry in order to spend a few
hours with him and to comfort him, and to urge
him to listen to reason. He described the visit in a
long and interesting letter to his daughter; our last
glimpse. He disliked Pondicherry: the only fine thing
in it was the sea with its long breakers which seemed
to say, "It's time we swallowed you up." He passed
the customs barrier, filled up various petty forms, and
found himself in "the crowded ramshackle bazaars
of the capital of French India": there was an occa-

sional tricolour and a notice "Ralentir" and a street called after Dupleix: otherwise it might have been any obscure little provincial town. He reached an old house in a side street: everything was old and dilapidated. The Maharajah of Dewas Senior awaited him in the doorway, barefooted, dressed in white. They entered, they sat on a sofa, and the Maharajah laid his head on his lap and burst into tears. "I put my arms round him, and O how thin he was. His eyes expressed nothing but wild tragic entreaty—entreaty for sympathy in all he has suffered. One great change is his beard. This is long and full and half grey."

Soon they got on to his "case" against the Government and then the eyes flashed and "almost started out of their sockets with defiance." He would concede nothing: "I am a Rajput and I should be false to all my traditions if I compromised my honour. I would much rather die here than do that." Malcolm "reasoned with him a little," pointed out that "the other side" was now ruling in Dewas, that he could not live in Pondicherry indefinitely and must think of his children and so on. He cried, "If I do not return to Dewas as absolute master my enemies will poison my children or myself. They will certainly do that."

Tea was then announced, and they went upstairs:

In a large upper room I found all his family. The room was just alive with children, mostly girls of all sizes, but there were three boys and two small grandchildren. The Maharani* was there of course and sat by me at tea. But the most striking was Prabhavati,† the one you fell in love with last year. She was dressed in a beautiful claret-coloured sari and held herself like a queen. She talked perhaps a shade too assertively for strict Indian custom: but that may be because I was looked upon as a member of the family and not one to be treated with any ceremony. "We have learnt many lessons here," she said, holding her neck almost defiantly high. "What?" I asked. "Sweet are the uses of adversity," she replied. "What use?" I continued. "Our geese are swans and our swans geese." An allusion to the many who have

----

* Bai Saheba now bore that title.

† Today she is an erudite Vedic scholar and an active politician. In the parliamentary elections of December 1951 she stood as a candidate for the Dewas region.

deserted them. At first they had no servants and the children had to do all the service.

After tea the children crowded round him, over-flowing with affection, the eldest boy "a clever deter-mined little monkey—so good looking too" clambered onto his chair and thrust the others away. Conversation turned to finance. The Maharajah was desperate for money. He had been selling jewels, but the French were on the *qui vive* against smuggling. Could anyone lend him a couple of thousand pounds? If the Government of India wouldn't "climb down" he meant to go to France or Japan: he had "resources for this" he said darkly. But he dare not re-enter British India, lest his freedom be restricted. Family dinner followed —a pleasant meal—and then the sad leave-taking. Bai Saheba wept and wept and implored to be delivered from Pondicherry: she and all the children loathed it. The Maharajah wept also, and Malcolm had a last word with him and implored him to make some concession, however small, which could be reported to the Viceroy at Delhi and form a basis for discussion; "I will think it over" was the useless reply.

On reaching the railway station, Malcolm looked

at his pass book, and sent back a cheque to the amount that he could afford; though, when he remembered that crowded upper room, it seemed like "sending an elephant a bun." On his return to Delhi he tried to see one of the Viceroy's chief advisers, but an interview was refused.

Two months later he heard disheartening rumours. According to a reliable informant, the retirement to Pondicherry had been premeditated; valuables had been despatched there beforehand, everything had gone there, down to the last poor symbols of royalty, even the silver trappings had been torn off the howdahs and had gone. Our appeals continued, but it was no good. He seemed bent on his own destruction. Perhaps he was destroying himself. In the May of 1935 Malcolm received a charming telegram alluding to "our subtly-bound claims on your affectionate care."

Then the darkness thickens, the distortions of disease and approaching dissolution increase, and in December 1937 Bapu Sahib died. His body was cremated according to his ancestral rites and his ashes were swallowed up by the sea.

✦

The *Times* of London duly carried an obituary notice of him. It is a model of ungenerosity and prim indignation and I read it with rage. The rage has subsided, for after all what else could the *Times* carry? Here was an Indian Ruler who had not been a success, who had maladministered his state and got into debt and given the Government of India trouble, who had not even been frank when invited by British officials to be so. "He came of an ancient and renowned dynasty, and in the early years of his rule gave some promise of doing well, but an ungovernable temper and self-indulgence led to serious deterioration." The progress of the deterioration is traced; his marriage and its failure, the departure of the Kolhapur Princess, his feud with her house, his troubles with his son are all described, not from his point of view, but the point of view of his enemies; his appeal to Ramsay MacDonald and his penitential fasts are sneered at. There is not one hint that he was lovable and brilliant and witty and charming, and (more exasperating still) not one hint that he was complex. He will go down to history as a failure. That is the sort of thing that does go down to history.

I am not concerned to rehabilitate his memory,

still less to present him as an object of pity: men have always misinterpreted the past and always will misinterpret it: the past must be left to its own dead who knew that it was alive. But I do offer him as a subject for study. From start to finish, from the days when he behaved well and was officially petted down to the days when he misbehaved and was punished, he was never simple, never ordinary, never deaf to the promptings which most of us scarcely hear. His religion was the deepest thing in him. It ought to be studied—neither by the psychologist nor by the mythologist but by the individual who has experienced similar promptings. He penetrated into rare regions and he was always hoping that others would follow him there. He was never exclusive, despite his endless pujahs. To recall the conversation that we had forty years ago in an upper room at Delhi, he was hopeful that we should all be recalled to the attention of God.

One of the puzzling things about the dead is that it is impossible to think of them evenly. They all go out of sight and are forgotten, they all go into silence, yet we cannot help assigning some of them a tune.

Most of those whom I have known leave no sound behind them; I cannot evoke them though I would like to. He has the rare quality of evoking himself, and I do not believe that he is here doing it for the last time.

Books by E. M. Forster
available in paperback editions
from Harcourt Brace Jovanovich, Inc.

ABINGER HARVEST

ASPECTS OF THE NOVEL

THE ETERNAL MOMENT AND OTHER STORIES

THE HILL OF DEVI

A PASSAGE TO INDIA

TWO CHEERS FOR DEMOCRACY

GOLDSWORTHY LOWES DICKINSON